Jenny Craig ®

healthy living
for life

my health and wellbeing
are worth the effort of making
new habits.

Jenny Craig ®

healthy living
for life

RECIPES FOR WEIGHT MANAGEMENT AND WELLBEING

MURDOCH BOOKS

Contents

DIP IN, clockwise from top left: tzatziki, hommus, eggplant dip and beetroot dip, pages 54–55

With every positive step
I take, I am wiser, stronger and
more confident.

Preface

At Jenny Craig, it's no surprise we're passionate about food. We think it, breathe it, sleep it — and of course we eat it! Whether we're creating new recipe concepts, tasting early prototypes, analysing the (very many) subsequent samples against our dietitians' strict guidelines and our clients' well-educated palates, or approving a product and then designing the menus, we love it. It's what we do, every day.

Our passion for food and our belief in the emotional and physical benefits of healthy eating led us to create this cookbook for anyone and everyone who appreciates delicious, nutritious food.

This is a collection of our favourite recipes, to be enjoyed by all the family as well as friends. If you're a Jenny Craig client, you can incorporate these recipes into your halfway or maintenance menu. Every recipe captures the natural flavours in our fresh produce, and features ingredients that are readily available in supermarkets — and every single dish can be prepared with the confidence of knowing that you'll be bringing wholesome, nourishing and wonderfully flavoursome food to the table.

When our clients are on our program, we encourage them to use their favourite spices, herbs and vegetables in their meals to suit their personal taste. Likewise, we also encourage you to experiment, adapt and 'tweak' the fabulous recipes in this book to make them your own. Your tastebuds are naturally adventurous, so why not offer them variety while you nourish your body and manage your weight?

With this cookbook we hope meals with friends, meals for special family occasions and those 'not so ordinary' everyday meals will become an enjoyable part of your life.

We ask only three things: firstly, that this cookbook doesn't become 'another one for the shelf'. Use it every day, once a week or maybe even once a month — but let it become the first book that you select each time you want to enjoy healthy food.

Secondly, 'personalise' it. Change ingredients to suit your own taste, write down these changes and make the recipes truly your own.

Finally, have fun and enjoy making these recipes. Share the pleasure of food with family and friends — together we can all make a difference and spread the passion for a healthier lifestyle.

Jenny Craig®

Welcome to healthy living

Since first opening in Melbourne, Australia, in 1983, Jenny Craig has been helping millions of people worldwide achieve their weight management goals by learning to live healthier lives.

With more than half of the population in Western countries now overweight or obese, there is no better time to get in shape and stay in shape.

The Jenny Craig Program

Jenny Craig offers a personalised approach to healthy weight loss and long-term weight maintenance. It is a comprehensive weight management program that incorporates kilojoule and portion-controlled ready-to-eat meals, as well as your own fresh fruit, vegetables, dairy, wholegrains and lean meat.

It teaches you how to eat a variety of foods in the right amounts, make physical activity a regular and enjoyable part of your lifestyle, and address many of the behaviours that can result in unwanted weight gain.

The program is designed by a team of highly qualified health practitioners including Accredited Practising Dietitians and an International Medical Advisory Board of renowned experts in the fields of nutrition, exercise physiology, lifestyle change, medicine and psychology. This team ensures our program offers the most effective weight-loss strategies for long-term weight management and lifestyle change, incorporating three key factors for weight management success.

The 3 keys to success

1   A healthy relationship with food
Our menus are based on the dietary guidelines for Australia and New Zealand and are well balanced, kilojoule-controlled and offer a wide variety of delicious foods. In addition to the Jenny Craig meals and snacks, you incorporate your own fresh ingredients with at least five serves per day of vegetables, two serves of fruit, as well as low-fat dairy products, lean meats, wholegrains and heart-healthy fats.

During the first half of the program, our model menu teaches you about correct portion sizes. Halfway through your program, your Jenny Craig consultant will teach you to start planning your own days, eating your own foods. You'll receive all the information you need to choose the right type of foods in the right amounts for one or two days of the week. By the time you complete the weight-loss component of the program, you'll be ready for seven days of self-planned eating.

2   Be active

To get the energy-balance equation right, you need to be burning some of the kilojoules your body takes in, which is why learning to incorporate more physical activity into your lifestyle is so important. To begin with, you will simply move a little more today than you did yesterday. As time goes on you'll enjoy making physical activity a regular part of your life because you'll be motivated by the positive feelings and improved well-being it brings!

You don't need to become an elite athlete — it's about finding an activity you enjoy for your level of fitness, and one that fits into your lifestyle. Your Jenny Craig consultant will assess your readiness to incorporate regular activity, and you will then set goals to achieve a level of physical activity that's just right for you and that you can maintain in the long term.

3   Support and encouragement

Every client is unique, so our program is tailored to suit individual tastes and needs. Your very own Jenny Craig consultant will meet with you privately each week to share your results and help you develop the skills you need to achieve and maintain your goals. Many of our personal consultants have been on the program themselves, and they know that success depends more on 'skill power' than 'will power'. Your one-on-one consultations will help you lose the weight and teach you how to manage your weight for life.

Helpful resource materials are provided every step of the way, and advice, assistance and support are readily available between consultations through our Customer Care line and our website.

What's the secret to losing weight and keeping it off?

There is no secret — it's all about having a healthy lifestyle. Choosing to eat a variety of foods in the right amounts, enjoying regular physical activity and having the right attitude are the cornerstones of long-term weight management success.

The key is to set realistic goals and not fall for the 'magic wand syndrome', trying every pill, potion, lotion and dietary fad that promises rapid weight loss. To lose weight and keep it off, you need to lose weight safely and slowly. That means around $1/2$–1 kg (1–2 lb) per week, or if you are over 100 kg (220 lb), not more than 1% of your body weight per week.

While all this sounds sensible, many people find adopting a healthy lifestyle much easier if they have some support — not only with the eating and exercising, but also the psychological aspects. Dealing with emotional issues without food can be difficult, especially for overweight people. So developing a healthy relationship with food is vital for long-term healthy weight management.

Weight management tips

Set realistic goals

It is important to set realistic goals that change your eating as well as your activity habits. Small changes — such as adding one fruit or vegetable to your typical daily diet, or using a pedometer (a small clip-on device that counts your steps as you walk) to build an extra 2000 more steps into your day — can add up to big results over time.

Watch out for portion distortion

Bring portions back into balance by using visual cues: a deck of cards equals a serving of meat or poultry, and a tennis ball equals a fruit serving. At meal times, serve individual plates rather than the tempting full spread on the table. You can also make portions look larger by using smaller plates.

Also practise 'slim' shopping strategies — plan meals and write a grocery list, never shop when hungry, and buy single-serve snack and dessert items.

Start the meal right

Start your meal with a salad, bowl of fruit or broth-based soup. You'll find that meals built on fruits, vegetables, wholegrains and soups may actually be more satisfying and result in fewer total kilojoules consumed.

If you're headed for a social event, don't leave the house too hungry. If you eat a healthy snack containing fruit and vegetables before the gathering, you'll be more likely to manage your temptations and less likely to overeat.

Cut kilojoules in the kitchen

To conserve kilojoules when cooking, think 'replace, reduce or remove'. Replace essential ingredients with low-fat options, like using low-fat yoghurt to replace cream, or using 1 cup of fruit purée to replace $1/2$ cup of oil when baking. For non-essential ingredients like nuts or chocolate chips, either reduce the amount, or completely remove the item from the recipe.

Include short bursts of activity

Look for ways to add up short bursts of activity every day — take the stairs, walk the dog, or ride a bicycle to the local shops. Aim for at least three lots of 10-minute activities each day.

Keep the variety alive

Mix up your workout routine with a combination of cardio, resistance and strength training. A balanced weekly workout includes cardio or aerobic activities to burn kilojoules and strengthen the heart; resistance activities to tone the muscles, maintain metabolism and bone health; and stretching activities for flexibility.

Don't let emotions run wild

When you find yourself craving a particular food, 'stop to decide', then work out whether to eat it or not. Decide what you'll eat by asking yourself whether it is true hunger that is driving you to eat, or more likely emotional eating.

If you still crave that food, decide to serve yourself a moderate portion to prevent yourself from overeating. Think about what you are doing and why. Decide to eat slowly, and allow 20 minutes to enjoy the food that you crave so much.

If you are not experiencing physical hunger, decide to leave the dining room or eating place and find an alternative to food.

Good nutrition tips

The aim of the Jenny Craig program is not just to help you lose weight, but to ensure you gain an understanding of good nutrition — after all, it's what's on the inside that counts as well. Here are some vital nutrition tips to get you started.

Wake up to breakfast

Studies show that people who skip breakfast end up gaining weight, not losing it. Breakfast is the most important meal of the day. The best way to start your day is with a high-fibre/low-sugar cereal and low-fat milk, or another combination of nutritious carbohydrates and lean protein. This can help stop you overeating later in the day.

Eat your greens — and reds, purples, oranges and blues!

Eating a variety of foods — especially vibrant-coloured fruits and vegetables — gives your body plenty of vitamins and antioxidants, which ensures your skin, hair and nails stay healthy, and keeps you feeling great. Aim for 20–30 different types of foods every day. This is easy to do with simple steps such as this: to meet your minimum daily two serves of fruit, rather than having two apples, consider perhaps an apple and say an orange.

Oils ain't oils

We all know we need to eat less fat when we are trying to lose weight, because fat has more kilojoules per gram than sugar, protein and even alcohol. However, we need to make a distinction between saturated fat (the kind that clogs up your arteries) and the unsaturated types such as the omega-3s and mono-unsaturated fats, which are good for heart health.

Some researchers believe that the good fats like those found in oily fish, avocados, nuts, seeds and oils such as olive oil may not be metabolised in the same way as the saturated and trans fats found in fatty meats, full-cream dairy, lard, pies, pastries and biscuits. So even if you are trying to lose weight, include some of the healthy fats — your skin, joints and heart will love you for it!

Stay fresh with water

Your body needs a constant supply of water to stay well hydrated. As the most important essential nutrient, water is vital for transporting nutrients to the cells, the proper functioning of the kidneys and lungs, as well as digestion and regulating our body temperature.

Water also helps in weight loss. It's amazing how often a glass of water will be exactly what's needed to satisfy a 'hunger' that was in fact simply thirst. Try sipping water with a sprig of mint, a slice of citrus or a berry or two for a zero-kilojoule refreshing drink.

What about the kids?

As you glance through this book, you'll notice that we have incorporated recipes that are family friendly. After all, we know our population has an increasing obesity rate, and we can all contribute to stop this emerging and alarming trend.

With our kids, fast food has been blamed, along with long hours spent sitting in front of the TV or computer, but in truth genetic and many environmental factors determine whether children lose or gain weight. It all comes back to balancing the kilojoules gained from food against the kilojoules used up during the day in our overall physical activity.

The most powerful influence you can have on the weight of your child is to maintain your own weight in the healthy weight range. Role modelling a healthy lifestyle has a flow-on effect: when one family member makes the change, often others do too, including the family dog!

Let's look at some handy tips to get your kids (or grandkids) helping out in the kitchen and interested in good nutrition.

Kids in the kitchen

A great way to start your kids on the path to healthy eating is to get them interested in food preparation as early as possible. This establishes great life skills — and you may also find you have a budding celebrity chef in the wings!

There's so much for kids to learn about food and nutrition, but how do you get them involved without ending up in fights, mess and a delayed dinner?

Try these great tips and ideas for fun food projects to suit all ages.

Time it right
Dinner time can be one of the most stressful times to have little hands helping out, so why not:
- make muffins or pancakes for a leisurely Sunday brunch
- try easy options like making your own pizzas where you can prepare toppings such as chargrilled vegetables and grated cheese in advance
- get kids going on fruit salad for dessert with a plastic picnic knife as you make the main course.

Mix it up
No-one likes mess in the kitchen, but it's important not to be too regimented about meals and to maintain variety:
- move it outside on a balmy evening and eat picnic style in the backyard or local park
- make fruit faces together at snack time – try blueberry eyes, watermelon smiles, kiwi fruit cheeks and starfruit hair, or try threading fruit kebabs
- have a cuisine 'theme night' where you go Spanish, Mexican, Italian or Japanese. Set the table to your theme, play some appropriate music and talk about different cultures and eating styles.

Make a kitchen classroom
Chances are you have your kids around the kitchen bench or table with afterschool homework, so look for ways to link back to food and nutrition too:
- get them to decorate individual recipe books where they can list their food preferences and favourite dishes
- teach your kids where food comes from by growing herbs or cherry tomato pots together
- go straight to the source and try strawberry picking or visiting a farmers' market.

Teen scene

If you have teenagers in your family, ask them to read this page and get the whole family talking about nutrition and the importance of healthy weight management.

No carbs, no go

Don't believe the fad diets and popular celebrity weight-loss stories that say avoiding carbohydrates will make you lose lots of weight. Carbohydrates are essential for your body and for good health. They are the best source of fuel for your muscles and brain — they help you concentrate, and give you energy for sport and play. Choose good carbohydrates like wholegrain bread, pasta, rice, breakfast cereal and fruit, as well as starchy vegetables like corn and potatoes, pumpkin and peas.

Reach your peak with calcium

It's a myth that dairy foods are fattening. The calcium in dairy foods is important for building strong bones and healthy teeth and making sure that you reach your peak growth. Eating three or four serves of dairy foods a day — like reduced-fat milk, cheese and yoghurt — is the best way to meet your calcium needs without unwanted saturated fat and kilojoules.

Sweat it out

The Physical Activity Recommendations for Children and Youth recommend 60 minutes of moderate to vigorous-intensity physical activity each day. So choose a sport you love, sign up for an activity class, or find a daily activity like a circuit run at your local park to get your blood pumping and keep you fit and healthy.

Go easy on the box

The Physical Activity Recommendations for Children and Youth also recommend that you spend no more than two hours per day using electronic media for entertainment. So put a stopwatch on your TV, computer games and web time (unless it's for homework of course!) and move it outdoors as much as you can.

Be positive and encourage a positive body image

Remember that healthy people come in all shapes and sizes. You grow and mature in bursts, and often at different times to your friends. Healthy eating, regular physical activity and a positive attitude help grow a happy, healthy mind and body and will help get you through these exciting, challenging years.

Using the Jenny Craig cookbook

This cookbook has been designed for anyone interested in managing their weight and adopting healthy eating habits. Whether you're a Jenny Craig member or just want some tasty, nutritious new recipe ideas, there's something for everyone in the family, for every meal of the day. As well, we think you'll love the 'Spice it up' section which allows you to add a personal touch to just about any of your meals. We've included recipes for those on the go, as well as for times when you want to create a little more passion in the kitchen. You'll also see we've included tips for preparation, storage, time savers and nutrition, to help you get the best out of the effort that you put in.

Every recipe has been tested in a homestyle kitchen setting using readily available ingredients. If you're interested in the nutritional content of each recipe, you'll find it in the top corner, outlining the kilojoules, protein, total fat, saturated fat, carbohydrate and fibre per serving. If you are on the Jenny Craig program you will find the Food Groups table (page 184 onwards) to be of particular value when you begin to plan your own meals.

Entertaining for family and friends

Whether you're on the Jenny Craig program or not, managing your weight doesn't mean putting your social life on hold. This cookbook will take the stress out of entertaining by helping you prepare healthy and delicious meals incorporating lots of fresh ingredients, colours and textures. You can prove that healthy food really does taste great — and also that we can enjoy delightful desserts and still manage our weight! You'll be amazed by the positive comments you'll get — and do use the serving sizes suggested, as so often we eat far more than we need.

Create your own delicious menu, or try the suggestions included with many of our recipes. Why not start with a mix of dips (pages 54–55) served with a wonderful array of vegetable crudités and toasted pitta bread? Next serve up a flavoursome creamy potato soup (page 64), or a warm chicken salad (page 46). Then select a main meal that you can serve with platters of delicious vegetables from the selection of sides for all to share. The peppered beef on potato mash (page 121) or poached salmon with mango salsa (page 102) are sure to delight, served up with a tomato basil salad (page 128), and asparagus and green beans with toasted almonds (page 132). Finish with a delicious passionfruit bavarois (page 157) or white chocolate mousse (page 166) and your guests will leave giving full compliments to the chef.

Whether you're a weight management enthusiast, or just looking for some new food ideas, we do hope you'll find what you're looking for — so please cook and enjoy!

start your day

Research tells us that people who eat breakfast are less likely to overeat during the rest of the day. And that means a greater chance of success with maintaining a healthy weight. We also know that a nutritious breakfast helps with concentration and learning ability. So what's stopping you? Start your day the right way!

bircher muesli

Serves 4

PER SERVE	
KILOJOULES	1344 (320 CAL)
PROTEIN	16.1 g
FAT	6.4 g
SATURATED FAT	0.9 g
CARBOHYDRATE	46.3 g
FIBRE	5.9 g

In a large bowl, mix together the oats, yoghurt, milk, currants and almonds. Cover and refrigerate overnight.

Just before serving, stir in the apple and strawberries, reserving some as a garnish.

Serve cold, with extra milk stirred through.

- 150 g (5^1/$_2$ oz/1^1/$_2$ cups) rolled (porridge) oats
- 500 g (1 lb 2 oz) plain fat-free yoghurt
- 250 ml (9 fl oz/1 cup) low-fat milk, plus extra, to serve
- 2 tablespoons currants
- 1 tablespoon slivered almonds
- 2 apples, grated
- 250 g (9 oz/1^1/$_3$ cups) chopped strawberries

cook's tip Substitute finely chopped dried apricots for the currants, and chopped pistachio nuts for the almonds

nutrition tip Excellent source of vitamin C and calcium

mango maple
smoothie

Serves 4

PER SERVE	
KILOJOULES	867 (206 CAL)
PROTEIN	12.1 g
FAT	0.7 g
SATURATED FAT	0.2 g
CARBOHYDRATE	36.3 g
FIBRE	2.3 g

- 3 ripe medium mangoes
- 400 g (14 oz) low-fat vanilla yoghurt
- 1 tablespoon maple syrup
- 500 ml (17 fl oz/2 cups) chilled skim milk

Remove the flesh from the mangoes and place in a blender. Add the yoghurt, maple syrup and milk.

Blend until frothy and well combined, then pour into four chilled glasses and serve.

cook's tip If fresh mangoes are not available, use 500 g (1 lb 2 oz/1⅔ cups) tinned mango and 200 g (7 oz/1 cup) tinned peaches instead

nutrition tip Excellent source of vitamin C and calcium

storage tip Remove the skin and stones from fresh, ripe mangoes and store the flesh in freezer bags, ready for use all year round

sourdough toasts with crispy ham

Serves 4

PER SERVE	
KILOJOULES	1184 (282 CAL)
PROTEIN	21.2 g
FAT	6.3 g
SATURATED FAT	1.9 g
CARBOHYDRATE	32 g
FIBRE	5.3 g

Preheat the grill (broiler) to medium–high. Sit the tomatoes, cut side up, on a large baking tray with the mushrooms, then lightly spray with the olive oil spray. Season well with freshly ground black pepper. Grill for 5–8 minutes, or until cooked, adding the ham during the last 2–3 minutes so it becomes slightly crispy.

Combine the cottage cheese, parsley and chives. Spread thickly over four of the toast slices and arrange the tomatoes, ham and mushrooms over the top. Drizzle with a little balsamic vinegar and top with the remaining toast slices.

- 4 roma (plum) tomatoes, cut in half
- 8 button mushrooms, sliced
- olive oil spray
- 8 slices of 97% fat-free ham
- 160 g (5¾ oz/⅔ cup) low-fat cottage cheese
- 2 tablespoons chopped flat-leaf (Italian) parsley
- 1 tablespoon snipped chives
- 8 slices of a small loaf of sourdough bread (preferably wholegrain), cut thickly at an angle and toasted
- balsamic vinegar, for drizzling

vegetarian Replace the ham with caramelized onions (see page 143)

cook's tip Instead of the sourdough you could use rye bread or ciabatta, a dense, crusty Italian bread available from most bakeries and delicatessens

nutrition tip Excellent source of vitamin C

berry yoghurt smoothie

Serves 4

PER SERVE	
KILOJOULES	272 (65 CAL)
PROTEIN	5.5 g
FAT	0.3 g
SATURATED FAT	0.1 g
CARBOHYDRATE	8.9 g
FIBRE	2.2 g

- 250 g (9 oz) low-fat strawberry yoghurt
- 125 ml (4 fl oz/$1/2$ cup) chilled cranberry juice
- 250 g (9 oz/$12/3$ cups) strawberries, hulled and chopped
- 125 g ($41/2$ oz/1 cup) frozen raspberries

Put the yoghurt and cranberry juice in a blender and pulse to combine. Add the strawberries and most of the frozen raspberries, then blend until smooth.

Pour into four chilled glasses and top with the remaining frozen raspberries. Serve with a spoon as the smoothie is quite thick.

nutrition tip Excellent source of vitamin C

cook's tip If fresh strawberries are not in season, use any frozen berries of your choice

crunchy oats 'n' all

PER SERVE	
KILOJOULES	1339 (319 CAL)
PROTEIN	12.5 g
FAT	10.2 g
SATURATED FAT	2.6 g
CARBOHYDRATE	40.4 g
FIBRE	8.2 g

Makes 15 servings of cereal

Preheat the oven to 170°C (325°F/Gas 3). Line a large baking tray with baking paper.

Toast the sesame seeds in a heated non-stick frying pan over medium heat for 30 seconds or until lightly golden, shaking the pan frequently. Tip into a small bowl and set aside.

In the same pan, toast the almonds for 30 seconds or until just starting to brown, shaking the pan often. Add the sunflower seeds, oats, cashews and coconut. Reduce the heat to low and stir for 2 minutes just to heat through, without browning. Remove the pan from the heat and stir in the toasted sesame seeds, honey and cinnamon. Stir well to coat all the ingredients with the honey.

Spread the oat mixture onto the prepared tray and bake for 15 minutes, or until it takes on a golden brown colour — be careful not to overcook. Stir once or twice during cooking so that the mixture browns evenly. Remove the tray from the oven and allow the mixture to cool completely on the tray. Mix the currants through and store in an airtight container.

To serve, arrange the fruit in a bowl or bowls, top with the yoghurt and sprinkle with 30 g (1 oz/1/3 cup) of the oat mixture.

CEREAL
- 2 1/2 tablespoons sesame seeds
- 3 tablespoons slivered almonds
- 3 tablespoons sunflower seeds
- 200 g (7 oz/2 cups) rolled (porridge) oats
- 2 1/2 tablespoons chopped cashew nuts
- 40 g (1 1/2 oz/2/3 cup) shredded coconut
- 2 1/2 tablespoons honey
- 1 teaspoon cinnamon
- 3 tablespoons currants

TO SERVE (PER SERVING)
- 150 g (5 1/2 oz/1 cup) chopped fresh fruit
- 100 g (3 1/2 oz) fat-free plain yoghurt

nutrition tip Excellent source of vitamin C. One serve contains over one-quarter of the daily adequate intake of dietary fibre

serving tip Use two or three different varieties of seasonal fresh fruit such as berries, kiwi fruit, banana, pear, apple, papaya, melon or stonefruits

banana and oat pikelets

PER SERVE	
KILOJOULES	1600 (381 CAL)
PROTEIN	14.8 g
FAT	5.2 g
SATURATED FAT	0.8 g
CARBOHYDRATE	65 g
FIBRE	5.9 g

Serves 4 (makes 16 pikelets)

- 140 g (5 oz/1 heaped cup) plain (all-purpose) flour
- 3 teaspoons baking powder
- 70 g (2$^1/_2$ oz/$^1/_2$ cup) oat bran
- 1 tablespoon caster (superfine) sugar
- 200 g (7 oz) fat-free yoghurt
- 120 g (4$^1/_4$ oz/$^1/_2$ cup) mashed banana
- 3 teaspoons light olive oil
- 1 teaspoon natural vanilla extract
- 4 egg whites (from 60 g/2 oz eggs)
- 2 bananas, extra, sliced
- 1 tablespoon honey

Sift the flour and baking powder into a large bowl. Stir in the oat bran and sugar.

In a separate bowl, mix together the yoghurt, mashed banana, olive oil, vanilla and 150 ml (5 fl oz) water. Tip the yoghurt mixture into the flour mixture and mix until just combined.

Using electric beaters, beat the egg whites into firm peaks — this will take about 1 minute. Stir one-third of the egg white through the pikelet batter, then fold the remaining egg white through.

Heat a large non-stick frying pan over medium heat. Spoon 60 ml (2 fl oz/$^1/_4$ cup) of the batter per pikelet into the hot pan (you should be able to cook three or four at a time). Cook for 2 minutes, or until bubbles appear on the surface, then flip each pikelet and cook for a further 1$^1/_2$ minutes, or until lightly golden underneath. Keep the pikelets warm in a moderate oven while cooking the remaining batter.

Serve warm with some banana slices and a drizzle of honey.

serving tip Delicious topped with smooth ricotta cheese, a drizzle of maple syrup and a sprinkle of cinnamon

sweetcorn and ricotta fritters

Serves 4 (makes 12 fritters)

PER SERVE	
KILOJOULES	1415 (337 CAL)
PROTEIN	18.9 g
FAT	10.9 g
SATURATED FAT	5 g
CARBOHYDRATE	37.1 g
FIBRE	7.4 g

Put the ricotta, egg, egg white and milk in a bowl and beat together until smooth. Stir in the flour, corn, spring onion and chives. Season well with freshly ground black pepper.

Spray a non-stick frying pan with olive oil spray. Add a heaped tablespoon of the fritter mixture to the pan, four at a time, and flatten to about 1.5 cm (5/8 inch) thick. Cook for 3–4 minutes on each side, then remove and drain on paper towels.

Serve the fritters in a stack of three, topped with a tablespoon each of ricotta and chutney.

- 200 g (7 oz/heaped 3/4 cup) low-fat ricotta cheese
- 1 egg
- 1 egg white
- 125 ml (4 fl oz/1/2 cup) skim milk
- 75 g (2 1/2 oz/1/2 cup) wholemeal (whole-wheat) self-raising flour
- 420 g (15 oz) tin no-added-salt corn kernels, drained
- 3 spring onions (scallions), chopped
- 2 tablespoons snipped chives
- olive oil spray
- 4 tablespoons low-fat ricotta cheese, extra
- 4 tablespoons ready-made spicy tomato chutney

nutrition tip Excellent source of calcium

cook's tip Instead of the tomato chutney, try the chilli relish on page 183. Also, use 2 fresh corn cobs if you prefer — simply cut away the kernels close to the cob using a sharp knife

PER SERVE	
KILOJOULES	1123 (267 CAL)
PROTEIN	6.6 g
FAT	4.2 g
SATURATED FAT	0.7 g
CARBOHYDRATE	46.8 g
FIBRE	7.3 g

mixed-grain porridge with rhubarb

Makes 16 servings of dry porridge mix
Makes 4 servings of stewed rhubarb

DRY PORRIDGE MIX

- 600 g (1 lb 5 oz/6 cups) rolled (porridge) oats
- 55 g (2 oz/^{1}/$_2$ cup) rolled rice flakes
- 60 g (2^1/$_4$ oz/^{1}/$_2$ cup) rolled barley
- 60 g (2^1/$_4$ oz/^{1}/$_2$ cup) rolled rye
- 30 g (1 oz/^{1}/$_4$ cup) millet flakes

STEWED RHUBARB

- 350 g (12 oz/7 stalks) rhubarb, trimmed, washed and cut into 5 cm (2 inch) lengths
- 1 apple, peeled, cored and chopped
- 100 g (3^1/$_2$ oz/^{1}/$_2$ cup) soft brown sugar
- ^{1}/$_4$ teaspoon ground mixed (pumpkin pie) spice

Put all the dry porridge mix ingredients in a large bowl and mix together well. Store in an airtight container until ready to use (will keep for up to 2 months).

To make enough porridge for 4 servings, put 2 cups of the porridge mixture in a saucepan with 1.25 litres (44 fl oz/5 cups) water. Bring to the boil, then reduce the heat and simmer, stirring frequently, over medium heat for 15 minutes, or until the porridge is thick. If it becomes too thick, add a little water (or skim milk).

Meanwhile, put all the ingredients for the stewed rhubarb in a saucepan with 250 ml (9 fl oz/1 cup) water. Slowly bring to the boil, stirring to dissolve the sugar. Reduce the heat and simmer for 10 minutes, or until the rhubarb is tender, stirring often. Serve hot or cold with the porridge.

time savers Using quick-cooking (or one-minute) oats will greatly reduce the cooking time of the porridge. Also, instead of the stewed rhubarb, top the porridge with 3 or 4 moist prunes

italian-style mini omelettes

Serves 6 (makes 12)

PER SERVE	
KILOJOULES	610 (145 CAL)
PROTEIN	12.7 g
FAT	9.6 g
SATURATED FAT	4.8 g
CARBOHYDRATE	2 g
FIBRE	0.6 g

Preheat the oven to 200°C (400°F/Gas 6). Lightly coat a 12-hole standard muffin tin with olive oil spray.

Cut the cherry tomatoes into quarters, squeeze out the seeds and dry the tomatoes on paper towels. Put the ricotta in a bowl and mash with a fork, then add the tomatoes, chives, half the parmesan, the beaten eggs and a little freshly ground black pepper. Mix together well. Whisk the egg whites until frothy ('small bubble' stage), then fold them through the ricotta mixture.

Spoon the mixture into the prepared muffin holes, sprinkle with the remaining parmesan and bake for 20 minutes, or until golden brown. Serve hot or at room temperature.

- olive oil spray
- 10 cherry tomatoes
- 300 g (10^1/$_2$ oz/1^1/$_4$ cups) reduced-fat fresh ricotta cheese
- 2 tablespoons finely snipped chives
- 4 tablespoons grated parmesan cheese
- 3 eggs, lightly beaten
- 3 egg whites

serving tip Serve on a toasted wholegrain English muffin

cook's tip For a spicy twist, stir ^{1}/$_4$ teaspoon chilli powder into the egg mixture before baking

storage tip Leftover mini omelettes can be refrigerated in an airtight container for up to 24 hours

spinach and feta frittatas

Makes 6

PER FRITTATA	
KILOJOULES	311 (74 CAL)
PROTEIN	8.1 g
FAT	4.1 g
SATURATED FAT	1.9 g
CARBOHYDRATE	0.8 g
FIBRE	0.8 g

- olive oil spray
- 150 g (5^1/$_2$ oz) English spinach leaves, washed
- 1 garlic clove, crushed
- 2 eggs
- 2 egg whites
- 60 ml (2 fl oz/^{1}/$_4$ cup) skim milk
- 1 tablespoon finely grated parmesan cheese
- 70 g (2^1/$_2$ oz) low-fat feta cheese, cut into 1 cm (^{1}/$_2$ inch) cubes

Lightly coat a six-hole muffin tin with olive oil spray.

Preheat the oven to 200°C (400°F/Gas 6). Put the spinach and garlic in a saucepan over medium heat. Cover and steam for 3 minutes, or until the spinach has wilted. Allow the spinach to cool slightly, then squeeze out any excess liquid and roughly chop the leaves.

In a bowl, whisk together the eggs, egg whites, skim milk and parmesan. Stir in the spinach and season with freshly ground black pepper.

Spoon the mixture into the prepared muffin holes, filling each three-quarters full. Lightly press three feta cubes into the top of each frittata.

Bake for 15 minutes, or until the frittatas are golden and set. Serve immediately, as they will deflate quite quickly.

cook's tip Black pepper is a wonderful seasoning for most savoury dishes, especially when freshly ground. Many supermarkets sell little pepper mills filled with assorted peppercorns that you can simply grind over your meals

serving tip Serve on a toasted English muffin with grilled tomatoes

tropical fruit crush

PER SERVE	
KILOJOULES	390 (93 CAL)
PROTEIN	2.1 g
FAT	0.3 g
SATURATED FAT	0 g
CARBOHYDRATE	18.3 g
FIBRE	4.1 g

Serves 4

Put all the ingredients except the mint leaves in a blender and blend until smooth. Pour into four chilled glasses, garnish with mint leaves and serve.

- 3 kiwi fruit, peeled and sliced
- 90 g (3$1/4$ oz/$1/2$ cup) peeled and cored pineapple chunks
- 1 banana, peeled
- 250 ml (9 fl oz/1 cup) chilled no-added-sugar tropical fruit juice
- 2 ice cubes
- small mint leaves, to garnish

nutrition tip Excellent source of vitamin C

cook's tip You can substitute the fruits with your personal favourites

something light

Refreshingly light and bursting with flavour, these simple dishes are perfect to enjoy as a lunch or light evening meal. They're great on their own — and even better with a side serve of fresh vegetables or salad.

club sandwich 1

PER SERVE	
KILOJOULES	1693 (403 CAL)
PROTEIN	23.9 g
FAT	15.5 g
SATURATED FAT	3.3 g
CARBOHYDRATE	39.4 g
FIBRE	5.4 g

Serves 4

- 12 slices of fresh, soft wholegrain bread
- 1 tablespoon ready-made pesto
- 1 smoked chicken breast, thinly sliced
- 70 g (2^1/2 oz/2 cups) rocket (arugula) leaves
- ^{1}/2 ripe avocado, mashed
- 1 Lebanese (short) cucumber, peeled and thinly sliced

Lay four slices of bread on a chopping board (each sandwich will need three slices of bread). Top each slice with one-quarter of the pesto, one-eighth of the chicken and one-eighth of the rocket.

Place a second slice of bread on top and spread with the avocado. Layer each with one-quarter of the cucumber, then the remaining chicken and rocket.

Top each sandwich with a third slice of bread. Slice away the crusts and cut each sandwich into two fingers.

serving tip Serve with a mixed leafy green salad and cherry tomatoes

club sandwich 2

Serves 4

PER SERVE	
KILOJOULES	1432 (341 CAL)
PROTEIN	11.1 g
FAT	14 g
SATURATED FAT	2.5 g
CARBOHYDRATE	40.1 g
FIBRE	5.8 g

Lay four slices of bread on a chopping board (each sandwich will need three slices of bread). Spread each slice with one-third of the avocado, then top each with 1 teaspoon pine nuts, three slices of salami, then one-eighth of the spinach and basil.

Place a second slice of bread on top. Spread each slice with the relish, then top with the remaining spinach and basil.

Top each sandwich with a third slice of bread. Slice away the crusts and cut each sandwich into two fingers.

- 12 slices of fresh, soft wholegrain bread
- $1/2$ ripe avocado, mashed
- 1 tablespoon pine nuts
- 12 paper-thin slices of small chilli salami (20 g / $3/4$ oz in total)
- 90 g ($3^1/4$ oz/2 cups) baby English spinach leaves
- a handful of basil
- 2 tablespoons chilli relish (see page 183), or a ready-made relish of your choice

cook's tip Try chopped walnuts or macadamia nuts instead of pine nuts

vietnamese rice paper rolls

Serves 4 (makes 12 rolls)

PER SERVE	
KILOJOULES	1262 (300 CAL)
PROTEIN	26.7 g
FAT	3 g
SATURATED FAT	0.8 g
CARBOHYDRATE	39.5 g
FIBRE	2.9 g

To make the dipping sauce, put the fish sauce and sugar in a small bowl with 125 ml (4 fl oz/1/2 cup) warm water. Stir until the sugar has dissolved, then add the garlic, chilli and lemon juice. Refrigerate until cool, adding the spring onion just before serving.

Half-fill a large saucepan with water and bring to the boil. Add the pork, then cover and boil over gentle heat for 12–15 minutes, or until cooked through. Transfer to a plate and allow to cool, then cut into 24 thin strips.

Put the noodles in a bowl and add hot water to cover. Soak for 2 minutes, or until softened, then drain.

Place a sheet of rice paper in a large bowl of warm water until just softened. Carefully lift it from the water and place on a board or plate. Lay two pork strips next to each other along the middle of the rice paper. Sit two prawn halves on top, then a small amount of noodles, lettuce, mint, Vietnamese mint and bean sprouts. Lift the bottom of the rice paper over the filling, fold in the two sides, then roll up from bottom to top. Cover with a damp tea towel (dish towel) so the rice paper doesn't dry out.

Repeat with the remaining ingredients to make 12 rice paper rolls. Serve with the dipping sauce.

DIPPING SAUCE
- 1 teaspoon salt-reduced fish sauce
- 2 tablespoons caster (superfine) sugar
- 4 garlic cloves, finely chopped
- 1 large red chilli, finely sliced
- 3 tablespoons lemon juice
- 1 spring onion (scallion), finely sliced

ROLLS
- 200 g (7 oz) piece of lean pork fillet
- 40 g (1 1/2 oz) rice vermicelli noodles
- 12 large round rice paper sheets (about 22 cm/ 8 1/2 inches in diameter)
- 12 cooked prawns (shrimp), peeled, deveined and cut in half down the middle
- 80 g (2 3/4 oz/2 cups) shredded iceberg lettuce
- a very large handful of mint
- a very large handful of Vietnamese mint
- 100 g (3 1/2 oz/1 heaped cup) bean sprouts

time saver The dipping sauce and pork can be prepared a day ahead — cover and store separately in the refrigerator

warm chicken salad

PER SERVE	
KILOJOULES	1230 (293 CAL)
PROTEIN	32.9 g
FAT	15.7 g
SATURATED FAT	3.6 g
CARBOHYDRATE	4.6 g
FIBRE	1.5 g

Serves 4

- 500 g (1 lb 2 oz) boneless, skinless chicken breasts
- 1 tablespoon olive oil
- 1 garlic clove, crushed
- 1 red capsicum (pepper), sliced into strips
- 4 spring onions (scallions), cut on the diagonal into 2 cm (3/4 inch) lengths
- 1 tablespoon cashew nuts
- 100 g (3 1/2 oz) mixed salad leaves
- juice of 2 limes
- a handful of coriander (cilantro) leaves

MARINADE
- 1 tablespoon salt-reduced soy sauce
- 1/2 teaspoon sesame oil
- 2 teaspoons sweet chilli sauce

Trim all visible fat from the chicken, then slice the chicken into thin strips and place in a bowl. Mix together the marinade ingredients, pour the marinade over the chicken and toss until well coated. Cover and leave to marinate in the refrigerator for at least 1 hour.

Drain off any excess marinade from the chicken. Heat half the olive oil in a wok or non-stick frying pan over high heat and stir-fry the chicken for 3 minutes, or until browned. Remove from the pan and set aside.

Heat the remaining oil in the wok and add the garlic, capsicum, spring onion and cashews. Stir-fry for 2 minutes, then return the chicken to the wok and cook for a further 1 minute.

Arrange the salad leaves on four serving plates and top with the chicken mixture. Drizzle with plenty of lime juice, scatter with coriander leaves and serve immediately.

time saver Marinate the chicken the night before

serving tip Serve over cooked thin egg noodles

nutrition tip Excellent source of vitamin C

protein power salad

PER SERVE	
KILOJOULES	1460 (348 CAL)
PROTEIN	23.6 g
FAT	7.8 g
SATURATED FAT	1.4 g
CARBOHYDRATE	41.3 g
FIBRE	8.8 g

Serves 4

a large saucepan of water to the boil and cook the
according to the packet instructions until *al dente*.
rinse with cold water, then drain again. Place in a
bowl.

the green beans for 2 minutes, or until tender but still
hy. Refresh under cold running water, then drain well.
the pasta with the remaining salad ingredients and
toss together.

dressing ingredients in a screw-top jar with some
ground black pepper and shake well to combine.
efore serving, shake the dressing again and pour all
he salad.

- 150 g (5^1/$_2$ oz/1^2/$_3$ cups) small pasta shapes of your choice
- 200 g (7 oz) green beans, cut into 5 cm (2 inch) lengths
- 200 g (7 oz/^{2}/$_3$ cup) tinned kidney beans, rinsed and drained
- 200 g (7 oz/^{2}/$_3$ cup) tinned chickpeas, rinsed and drained
- 185 g (6^1/$_2$ oz/1 cup) tinned tuna in springwater, drained
- a small handful of flat-leaf (Italian) parsley

DRESSING
- 1 tablespoon olive oil
- 2 tablespoons white wine vinegar
- 1 garlic clove, crushed
- 1 tablespoon wholegrain mustard

trition tip Good source of
hin C and iron (non-haem)

time saver This salad can be made a day
ahead — pour the dressing over just before serving

tandoori lamb salad

PER SERVE	
KILOJOULES	950 (226 CAL)
PROTEIN	31 g
FAT	5 g
SATURATED FAT	2.1 g
CARBOHYDRATE	13.1 g
FIBRE	2.3 g

Serves 4

- 250 g (9 oz) low-fat plain yoghurt
- 2 garlic cloves, crushed
- 2 teaspoons grated fresh ginger
- 2 teaspoons ground turmeric
- 2 teaspoons garam masala
- $1/4$ teaspoon paprika
- 2 teaspoons ground coriander
- 500 g (1 lb 2 oz) lean lamb loin fillets
- 150 g ($5^1/2$ oz) mixed salad leaves
- 1 large mango, cut into strips
- 2 cucumbers, sliced into half-moons
- 4 tablespoons lemon juice
- $1^1/2$ teaspoons chopped coriander (cilantro)
- 1 teaspoon chopped mint

In a bowl, mix together the yoghurt, garlic, ginger and spices. Add the lamb fillets and turn them about until thoroughly coated. Cover and refrigerate for at least an hour, or preferably overnight.

Preheat the grill (broiler) to high. Spread the lamb on a foil-lined baking tray and cook for 7 minutes on each side, or until the marinade starts to brown. Remove from the heat, cover loosely with foil and allow to rest for 5 minutes.

Put the salad leaves, mango and cucumber in a mixing bowl. Drizzle with the lemon juice and add the coriander and mint. Season with freshly ground black pepper, toss to combine, then arrange in four shallow bowls. Slice the lamb and serve over the salad.

serving tip Serve wrapped in pitta bread, with an extra dollop of plain low-fat yoghurt

nutrition tip Excellent source of vitamin C, iron and zinc

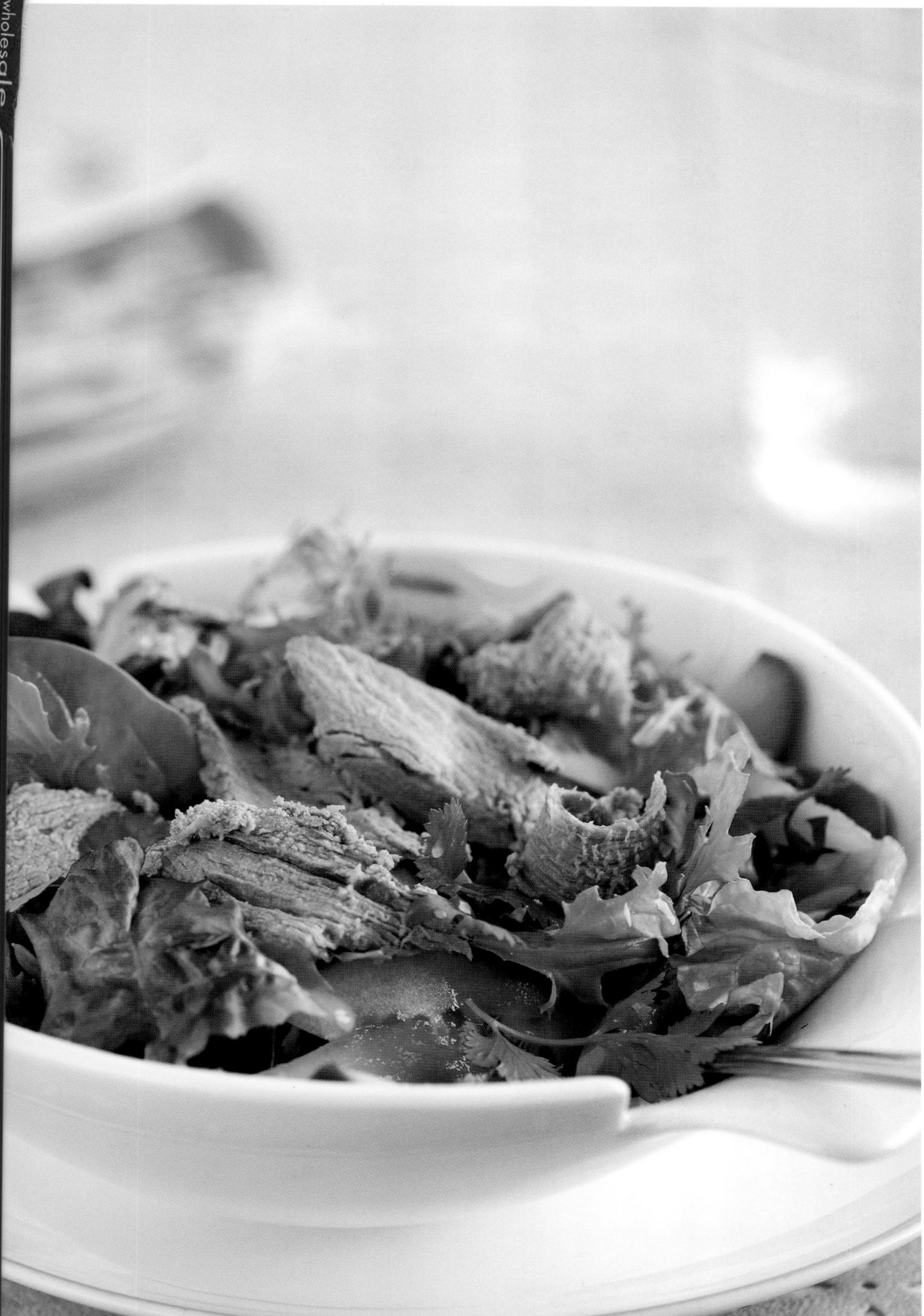

ons

PER SERVE	
KILOJOULES	797 (190 CAL)
PROTEIN	17 g
FAT	3.4 g
SATURATED FAT	1 g
CARBOHYDRATE	21.7 g
FIBRE	1.5 g

s 40 won tons)

ngredients in a large bowl and mix well.

apper on a work surface, and cover the
rs with a damp paper towel so they

easpoon of the filling in the centre of the
sten the edges with water. Fold the wrapper
triangle, enclosing the filling, then bring the
b and over to meet and slightly overlap at
where the edges overlap with egg white,
her to seal. Repeat with the remaining won
filling has been used. (Wrap any unused
tic wrap and freeze for up to 2 months.)

cepan of water to the boil. Add the won tons,
ut six, ensuring there is room for them to
y. Cook for 3 minutes, or until the filling is
Remove with a slotted spoon and drain well.
salt-reduced soy sauce or sweet chilli sauce.

FILLING

- 500 g (1 lb 2 oz) lean
  minced (ground) pork
- 1 carrot, grated
- 1 spring onion (scallion),
  finely chopped
- 2 garlic cloves, finely
  chopped
- 2 tablespoons salt-reduced
  oyster sauce
- 2 drops of sesame oil

- 1 packet of 9 cm (3^1/$_2$ inch)
  square won ton wrappers
- 1 egg white, lightly beaten
- salt-reduced soy sauce or
  sweet chilli sauce, to serve

time saver The won tons can be prepared
ahead of time up to the cooking stage and frozen for up
to 1 month — thaw in the refrigerator before cooking

PER SERVE	
KILOJOULES	140 (33 CAL)
PROTEIN	1 g
FAT	1.8 g
SATURATED FAT	0.2 g
CARBOHYDRATE	2.4 g
FIBRE	2 g

These four tasty dips can be served with fresh vegetable sticks, grilled Mediterranean vegetables, toasted wholemeal (whole-wheat) pitta bread or thinly sliced wholegrain sourdough, or as a low-fat sandwich spread.

eggplant dip

- 2 eggplants (aubergines)
- 1 garlic clove, crushed
- 1/2 teaspoon Indian curry powder
- 1/2 teaspoon ground cumin
- 2 teaspoons olive oil, approximately
- lemon juice, to taste
- chopped coriander (cilantro), to taste

Roast the whole eggplants (aubergines) in a 200°C (400°F/Gas 6) oven for 50 minutes — the flesh should be soft and the skin black and charred. Allow the eggplants to cool, then peel off the skin. Drain the flesh in a colander for 20 minutes to remove the excess liquid.

Put the eggplant in a food processor or blender with the garlic, curry powder and cumin. Slowly blend in enough olive oil to make the dip smooth. Season with freshly ground black pepper and add lemon juice and coriander to taste.

Serves 6

PER SERVE	
KILOJOULES	481 (115 CAL)
PROTEIN	3.5 g
FAT	8.4 g
SATURATED FAT	1.1 g
CARBOHYDRATE	5.3 g
FIBRE	2.6 g

hommus

Serves 8

- 300 g (10^1/2 oz) tin chickpeas
- juice of 1/2 lemon, plus extra, to taste
- 2 tablespoons olive oil
- 2 tablespoons tahini
- 2 garlic cloves, crushed

Rinse and drain the chickpeas well, then place in a food processor or blender with the remaining ingredients. Blend well, adding 2–3 tablespoons water as needed to make the dip smooth. Check the flavour and add a little more lemon juice if needed.

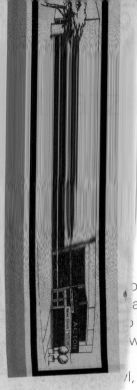

...ki

PER SERVE	
KILOJOULES	87 (21 CAL)
PROTEIN	2.1 g
FAT	0.1 g
SATURATED FAT	0 g
CARBOHYDRATE	2.5 g
FIBRE	0.4 g

...ers in half lengthways, scoop out the seeds ...ave the skin on and coarsely grate the ... a small colander. Sprinkle with salt and leave ...wl for 15 minutes to drain off any bitter juices.

...l, mix together the remaining ingredients.

...cumber under cold water then, taking small ..., squeeze out any excess moisture. Stir the cucumber into the yoghurt mixture and season well with freshly ground black pepper. Serve garnished with mint.

- 2 Lebanese (short) cucumbers
- 1/2 teaspoon salt
- 400 g (14 oz) low-fat plain yoghurt
- 4 garlic cloves, crushed
- 3 tablespoons finely chopped mint, plus extra, to garnish
- 1 tablespoon lemon juice

beetroot dip

Serves 8

PER SERVE	
KILOJOULES	76 (18 CAL)
PROTEIN	1 g
FAT	0 g
SATURATED FAT	0 g
CARBOHYDRATE	3.1 g
FIBRE	0.7 g

Blend all the ingredients in a blender until very smooth.

- 225 g (8 oz) tin beetroot (beets), drained well
- 80 g (2³/4 oz) fat-free plain yoghurt
- 1/2 teaspoon ground coriander
- 1 teaspoon ground cumin

mustard prawns with garlic

Serves 4

PER SERVE	
KILOJOULES	672 (160 CAL)
PROTEIN	26.2 g
FAT	3.3 g
SATURATED FAT	0.5 g
CRABOHYDRATE	0.8 g
FIBRE	0.9 g

- 2 teaspoons olive oil
- 4 garlic cloves, finely chopped
- 500 g (1 lb 2 oz) raw prawns (shrimp), peeled and deveined, tails intact
- 125 ml (4 fl oz/$\frac{1}{2}$ cup) white wine
- 2 tablespoons dijon mustard
- 2 tablespoons finely chopped parsley

Heat the olive oil in a frying pan over medium–high heat. Add the garlic and sauté for 30 seconds.

Add the prawns and cook, stirring, for 2 minutes. Stir in the wine and sauté for a further 2 minutes, or until the wine has reduced and the prawns curl up and have just turned pink. Reduce the heat, stir in the mustard, then sprinkle with the parsley and serve.

serving tip Serve on a bed of steamed long-grain rice with a large, leafy green salad

nutrition tip Good source of omega-3 fat

cook's tip Add a dash of honey during cooking, or toss fresh rocket (arugula) leaves through the prawns just before serving

crunchy noodle salad .

Serves 4

PER SERVE	
KILOJOULES	1720 (410 CAL)
PROTEIN	15.9 g
FAT	10.2 g
SATURATED FAT	1.5 g
CARBOHYDRATE	60.1 g
FIBRE	6 g

Cook the noodles in a large saucepan of boiling water for 4 minutes, or according to the packet instructions. Drain, rinse under cold running water and drain again.

Blanch the snow peas in boiling water for 1 minute. Drain, refresh under cold running water and drain again.

Put all the vegetables in a salad bowl and add the noodles. Put the lime and sesame dressing ingredients in a screw-top jar and shake well to combine. Just before serving, shake the dressing again and pour over the salad. Toss well.

- 300 g (10^1/$_2$ oz) thin egg noodles
- 125 g (4^1/$_2$ oz) snow peas (mangetout), trimmed and sliced lengthways
- 150 g (5^1/$_2$ oz/1^2/$_3$ cups) bean sprouts
- 50 g (1^3/$_4$ oz/heaped ^{3}/$_4$ cup) alfalfa sprouts
- 4 spring onions (scallions), sliced on the diagonal into 3 cm (1^1/$_4$ inch) lengths
- 1 red capsicum (pepper), cut into thin strips
- 150 g (5^1/$_2$ oz/3^1/$_3$ cups) shredded Chinese cabbage

LIME AND SESAME DRESSING
- 2 tablespoons salt-reduced soy sauce
- 4 tablespoons lemon or lime juice
- 1 tablespoon sesame oil
- 1 tablespoon sesame seeds
- 2 tablespoons (25 g/1 oz) unsalted peanuts, crushed
- 2 teaspoons soft brown sugar

cook's tip Add some cooked shredded chicken, prawns (shrimp) or boiled egg

nutrition tip Excellent source of vitamin C

thai beef salad

PER SERVE	
KILOJOULES	1514 (360 CAL)
PROTEIN	46.1 g
FAT	12.3 g
SATURATED FAT	4.6 g
CARBOHYDRATE	13.8 g
FIBRE	5 g

- 600 g (1 lb 5 oz) piece of lean beef fillet
- 2 teaspoons olive oil
- 70 g (2^1/$_2$ oz/1^1/$_2$ cups) baby English spinach leaves
- 1 red capsicum (pepper), cut into thin strips
- 1 Lebanese (short) cucumber, cut in half, then thinly sliced on the diagonal
- 100 g (3^1/$_2$ oz/1 heaped cup) bean sprouts
- 500 g (1 lb 2 oz) cherry tomatoes, cut in half
- ^{1}/$_2$ red onion, finely sliced
- a handful of coriander (cilantro) leaves
- a handful of mint

CHILLI LIME DRESSING
- 3 tablespoons sweet chilli sauce
- 3 tablespoons lime juice
- 2 teaspoons salt-reduced soy sauce
- 2 garlic cloves, finely chopped

Serv

Heat a chargrill pan or barbecue grill to high. Brush the with the olive oil, then cook for 3–4 minutes on each si medium–rare, or until done to your liking. Transfer to a cover loosely with foil and allow to rest for 15 minutes. the beef across the grain into thin strips, then set aside

In a large bowl, toss together the remaining salad ingre

Put the chilli lime dressing ingredients in a screw-top ja shake well.

Divide the salad among four plates, then arrange the b slices over the top and drizzle with the dressing.

serving tip Toss cooked thin rice noodles through the salad for extra carbohydrate and energy

nutrition tip Excellent source of vitamin C, iron and zinc

hearty corn soup

PER SERVE	
KILOJOULES	896 (213 CAL)
PROTEIN	9.4 g
FAT	3.8 g
SATURATED FAT	0.7 g
CARBOHYDRATE	31.8 g
FIBRE	7.2 g

Serves 6

Heat the olive oil in a large saucepan over medium heat. Add the onion, bacon, capsicum and chilli and sauté for 5 minutes, or until the onion and capsicum are soft.

Add the stock and potatoes and simmer for 15 minutes, or until the potato is cooked. Stir in the corn and cook for a further 5 minutes.

Remove from the heat and allow the soup to cool a little, then transfer to a blender and briefly process in batches, until just smooth but still quite thick and chunky.

Pour the soup back into the saucepan and gently reheat. Stir in the coriander or parsley just before serving.

Garnish with some extra coriander leaves if desired.

- 2 teaspoons olive oil
- 1 red onion, roughly chopped
- 2 slices of lean bacon, trimmed of rind and fat, then finely diced
- 1 red capsicum (pepper), chopped
- 1 red chilli, seeded and finely chopped
- 1.5 litres (52 fl oz/6 cups) salt-reduced vegetable stock
- 600 g (1 lb 5 oz) desiree or other all-purpose potatoes, skin on, diced
- 2 x 310 g (11 oz) tins no-added-salt corn kernels, drained
- 3 tablespoons finely chopped coriander (cilantro) or parsley

serving tip Serve with warm sourdough bread

storage tip Freeze any leftover soup in an airtight container for up to 1 month

nutrition tip Excellent source of vitamin C

creamy potato soup

PER SERVE	
KILOJOULES	1168 (278 CAL)
PROTEIN	14.2 g
FAT	2.9 g
SATURATED FAT	0.5 g
CARBOHYDRATE	45.8 g
FIBRE	5 g

Serves 4

- 2 teaspoons olive oil
- 1 onion, chopped
- 2 garlic cloves, chopped
- 1/2 teaspoon dried thyme
- 1 teaspoon ground coriander
- 4 large potatoes (about 800 g/1 lb 12 oz in total), peeled and chopped
- 200 g (7 oz) orange sweet potato, peeled and chopped
- 500 ml (17 fl oz/2 cups) salt-reduced chicken or vegetable stock
- 375 ml (13 fl oz/1 1/2 cups) low-fat evaporated milk
- 2 tablespoons fresh thyme, to serve

Heat the olive oil in a large saucepan over medium heat. Add the onion and garlic and sauté for 5 minutes, or until the onion is soft.

Add the dried thyme, ground coriander, potato, sweet potato, stock and 500 ml (17 fl oz/2 cups) water. Bring to the boil, then reduce the heat, cover and simmer for 20 minutes, or until the potato is tender.

Purée the soup using a hand-held blender or a food processor until just roughly blended. Return to a clean saucepan and stir in the milk and some freshly ground black pepper to taste. Gently reheat, then ladle into four warm bowls and sprinkle with fresh thyme.

nutrition tip Excellent source of vitamin C

serving tip Serve with warm pide (Turkish/flat bread) and hommus (see page 54). Stir through 1/2 bunch of finely chopped parsley for extra flavour and vitamin C

storage tip Keeps in the fridge for up to 3 days, or can be frozen for up to 1 month

ribollita (tuscan bread soup)

Serves 6

PER SERVE	
KILOJOULES	625 (149 CAL)
PROTEIN	8 g
FAT	4.3 g
SATURATED FAT	1.4 g
CARBOHYDRATE	16.6 g
FIBRE	6.1 g

If using dried beans, soak them in a bowl of cold water with the bay leaf overnight.

Heat the olive oil in a large saucepan, add the onion and garlic and sauté for 5 minutes, or until the onion is soft. Add the celery, carrot, chilli flakes and bacon and sauté for a further 5 minutes.

If using the soaked beans, drain them, remove the bay leaf and add to the saucepan with the tomato, cabbage, thyme and stock. Bring to the boil, then cover and simmer for 50 minutes, or until the beans are tender. (If using the tinned beans, first add the tomato, cabbage, thyme and stock to the saucepan, simmer for 20 minutes, then add the tinned beans and simmer for a further 25 minutes.)

Slice the crust off the bread, then break the bread into chunks and add to the soup. Cook for a further 10 minutes — the soup should be thick, but not dry. If necessary, ladle in some extra stock or water, 125 ml (4 fl oz/$\frac{1}{2}$ cup) at a time, during cooking.

Serve sprinkled with parmesan and some freshly ground black pepper.

- 150 g (5$\frac{1}{2}$ oz/$\frac{3}{4}$ cup) dried cannellini beans, or 400 g (14 oz) tin cannellini beans, rinsed and drained
- 1 bay leaf (optional)
- 2 teaspoons olive oil
- 1 onion, chopped
- 3 garlic cloves, chopped
- 3 celery stalks, chopped
- 2 carrots, chopped
- a pinch of chilli flakes
- 1 lean slice of bacon, trimmed of fat, then finely diced
- 400 g (14 oz) tin no-added-salt crushed tomatoes
- 150 g (5$\frac{1}{2}$ oz/2 cups) finely sliced cabbage
- 2 fresh thyme sprigs, or $\frac{1}{2}$ teaspoon dried thyme
- 2 litres (70 fl oz/8 cups) salt-reduced chicken or vegetable stock
- 100 g (3$\frac{1}{2}$ oz) stale loaf of Italian-style or sourdough bread
- 4 tablespoons grated parmesan cheese

storage tip Freeze any leftover soup in an airtight container for up to 1 month

curried vegetable soup

Serves 4

PER SERVE	
KILOJOULES	886 (211 CAL)
PROTEIN	11.6 g
FAT	5.6 g
SATURATED FAT	0.8 g
CARBOHYDRATE	23.9 g
FIBRE	9.2 g

- 1 tablespoon olive oil
- 1 onion, chopped
- 3–4 teaspoons mild curry powder, to taste
- 1 teaspoon ground cumin
- 1 litre (35 fl oz/4 cups) salt-reduced chicken or vegetable stock
- 2 tablespoons low-salt tomato paste (concentrated purée)
- 125 g (4^1/$_2$ oz/^{1}/$_2$ cup) red lentils
- 125 g (4^1/$_2$ oz/2 cups) broccoli florets
- 1 potato, peeled and chopped
- 2 carrots, chopped
- 1 celery stalk, chopped
- 1 tablespoon chopped parsley

Heat the olive oil in a large saucepan over medium heat. Add the onion, stir in the curry powder and cumin and sauté for 5 minutes, or until the onion is soft.

Stir in the stock, tomato paste and lentils. Bring to the boil, then add the vegetables. Simmer for 25 minutes, or until the vegetables are tender, stirring occasionally. Season with freshly ground black pepper, ladle into four warm bowls and serve sprinkled with parsley.

nutrition tip Excellent source of vitamin C and a good source of iron (non-haem). One serve contains almost one-third of the daily adequate intake of dietary fibre

serving tip Serve with a crusty wholegrain roll

storage tip Keeps in the refrigerator for up to 3 days, or can be frozen

mediterranean fish soup

Serves 4

PER SERVE	
KILOJOULES	1249 (297 CAL)
PROTEIN	32.2 g
FAT	6.4 g
SATURATED FAT	1.3 g
CARBOHYDRATE	23.1 g
FIBRE	6.3 g

Heat the oil in a large saucepan over low heat. Add the onion, leek, garlic, bay leaf and marjoram. Cover and cook for 10 minutes, shaking the pan occasionally, until the onion is soft. Add the orange zest, wine, capsicum and tomato, then cover and cook for 10 minutes.

Stir in the tomato passata, stock and tomato paste. Bring to the boil, then reduce the heat and simmer, uncovered, for 15 minutes.

Cut the fish into bite-sized pieces and add to the soup. Cover and cook for 8 minutes, or until the fish is flaky and tender. Add half the parsley, then season to taste with freshly ground black pepper. Discard the bay leaf. Just before serving, sprinkle with the remaining parsley. Ladle into four warm bowls and serve with the warm bread rolls.

- 2 teaspoons olive oil
- 2 large onions, thinly sliced
- 1 leek, white part only, rinsed well and chopped
- 4 garlic cloves, finely chopped
- 1 bay leaf
- 1/2 teaspoon dried marjoram
- 1 teaspoon grated orange zest
- 2 tablespoons dry white wine
- 1 red capsicum (pepper), cut into bite-sized pieces
- 500 g (1 lb 2 oz) ripe tomatoes, chopped
- 125 ml (4 fl oz/1/2 cup) no-added-salt tomato passata (puréed tomatoes)
- 500 ml (17 fl oz/2 cups) salt-reduced fish stock
- 2 tablespoons salt-reduced tomato paste (concentrated purée)
- 500 g (1 lb 2 oz) skinless, boneless fish fillets, such as snapper, red mullet, blue-eye cod or ocean perch
- 3 tablespoons chopped parsley
- 4 wholegrain dinner rolls, warmed

nutrition tip Good source of omega-3 fat and an excellent source of vitamin C

cook's tip Fish cooks very quickly and becomes opaque and flaky when done

mushroom, ham and olive pizza

Serves 6

PER SERVE	
KILOJOULES	1182 (281 CAL)
PROTEIN	17.7 g
FAT	7.1 g
SATURATED FAT	3.1 g
CARBOHYDRATE	33.4 g
FIBRE	6.2 g

- 4 roma (plum) tomatoes, cut into quarters
- 7 g (^{1}/$_4$ oz) dry yeast or 15 g (^{1}/$_2$ oz) fresh yeast
- ^{1}/$_4$ teaspoon sugar
- 215 g (7^1/$_2$ oz/1^3/$_4$ cups) plain (all-purpose) flour
- 125 ml (4 fl oz/^{1}/$_2$ cup) skim milk
- 2 teaspoons olive oil
- 1 onion, thinly sliced
- 2 garlic cloves, crushed
- 750 g (1 lb 10 oz) mushrooms, sliced
- 250 g (9 oz/1 cup) low-fat ricotta cheese
- 4 slices of 97% fat-free ham, chopped
- 2 tablespoons sliced black olives
- small handful of fresh basil leaves

Preheat the oven to 210°C (415°F/Gas 6–7). Put the tomato quarters on a baking tray lined with baking paper, sprinkle with freshly cracked black pepper and bake for 20 minutes, or until the edges are starting to darken.

Stir the yeast and sugar into 3 tablespoons warm water until the yeast has dissolved. Cover and leave in a warm place until foamy. Sift the flour into a large bowl. Warm the milk, then stir into the flour with the yeast mixture and mix to a soft dough. Turn out onto a lightly floured surface and knead for 5 minutes. Place in a lightly oiled bowl, then cover and leave in a warm place for 40 minutes, or until doubled in size.

Meanwhile, heat the olive oil in a frying pan over medium heat and sauté the onion and garlic for 5 minutes, or until soft. Add the mushrooms and stir until they are soft and the liquid has evaporated. Leave to cool.

Turn the dough out onto a lightly floured surface and knead lightly. Roll out to a 35 cm (14 inch) circle and transfer to a lightly greased oven or pizza tray. Spread with the ricotta, leaving a border. Top with the mushrooms and ham, leaving a circle in the centre, and arrange the tomato and olives in the circle. Fold the dough edge over onto the mushroom and dust the edge with flour. Bake for 25 minutes, or until the crust is golden. Scatter with basil and serve.

serving tip Serve with a rocket salad (see page 124). Delicious topped with caramelized onions (see page 143)

nutrition tip Excellent source of vitamin C

the main event

When you think about a nutritionally well-balanced main meal, picture a plate half-filled with vegetables, one-quarter with high-protein foods and the remainder with carbohydrate-rich foods. The recipes that follow make this easy. All you need to do is decide which one you'll choose!

chicken stir-fry

Serves 4

PER SERVE	
KILOJOULES	1189 (283 CAL)
PROTEIN	35.6 g
FAT	13.2 g
SATURATED FAT	3.2 g
CARBOHYDRATE	4.4 g
FIBRE	3.1 g

Heat half the olive oil in a wok over high heat until hot. Add the chicken and stir-fry for 2–3 minutes, or until just cooked through. Remove from the wok and set aside.

Heat the remaining oil over medium–high heat. Add the onion and garlic and stir-fry for 1 minute, or until aromatic. Stir in the broccoli, cauliflower, oyster sauce and 2 tablespoons water, then cover and steam for 2–3 minutes, or until the vegetables are cooked but still crisp.

Return the chicken to the wok and stir-fry for a further minute. Remove from the heat and sprinkle with coriander.

- 1 tablespoon olive oil
- 600 g (1 lb 5 oz) boneless, skinless chicken breasts, cut into thin strips
- 1 onion, cut into thin wedges
- 2 garlic cloves, finely chopped
- 120 g ($4^1/4$ oz/2 cups) broccoli florets
- 250 g (9 oz/2 cups) cauliflower florets
- 1 tablespoon salt-reduced oyster sauce
- a small handful of coriander (cilantro) leaves

cook's tip Add some sliced fresh baby corn and sprinkle with raw cashew nuts

serving tip Serve with steamed long-grain rice and honeyed carrots (see page 135), or toss through cooked thin egg noodles

nutrition tip Excellent source of vitamin C

spring vegetable risotto

Serves 4

PER SERVE	
KILOJOULES	1644 (391 CAL)
PROTEIN	11.8 g
FAT	9.3 g
SATURATED FAT	3.4 g
CARBOHYDRATE	59 g
FIBRE	3.5 g

- 900 ml (31 fl oz) salt-reduced vegetable stock
- 1 tablespoon olive oil
- 2 small zucchini (courgettes), chopped
- 100 g (3^1/$_2$ oz/^{2}/$_3$ cup) butternut pumpkin (squash), peeled and cut into 1 cm (^{1}/$_2$ inch) cubes
- 60 g (2^1/$_4$ oz/^{1}/$_2$ cup) chopped green beans
- 30 g (1 oz/^{1}/$_2$ cup) small broccoli florets
- 50 g (1^3/$_4$ oz/^{1}/$_2$ cup) sliced sugar snap peas, or 80 g (2^3/$_4$ oz/^{1}/$_2$ cup) frozen peas
- 8 French shallots, finely sliced
- 2 garlic cloves, crushed
- 1 large carrot, finely diced
- 2 celery stalks, finely diced
- 275 g (9^3/$_4$ oz/1^1/$_4$ cups) risotto rice
- 100 ml (3^1/$_2$ fl oz) dry white wine
- 50 g (1^3/$_4$ oz/^{1}/$_2$ cup) grated parmesan cheese
- chopped parsley, to serve

Pour the stock into a small saucepan. Bring just to the boil, then reduce the heat and keep at a low simmer.

Heat 1 teaspoon of the olive oil in a large non-stick frying pan. Add the zucchini, pumpkin, beans and broccoli and sauté over medium heat for 4 minutes. Add the peas and cook for a further 5–6 minutes, or until the pumpkin is soft. Remove from the heat and set aside.

Add the remaining oil to a large heavy-based saucepan and sauté the shallot, garlic, carrot and celery over low heat for 3 minutes, or until soft but not browned. Stir in the rice and cook for 1 minute, or until the grains are mixed through.

Increase the heat to medium and stir in the wine. Once all the wine is absorbed, begin adding the simmering stock, a ladleful at a time, stirring constantly with a wooden spoon until absorbed. Keep stirring the rice and ladling in the stock until all the stock is absorbed and the grains are tender — this should take about 20 minutes.

Remove the risotto from the heat and vigorously stir most of the parmesan through to give a creamy texture. Gently mix the cooked vegetables through, then cover and leave to rest for 2 minutes. Serve in warm bowls sprinkled with cracked black pepper, chopped parsley and the remaining parmesan.

serving tip Serve with a mixed green salad

nutrition tip Excellent source of vitamin C

sweet potato and feta frittata

Serves 4

PER SERVE	
KILOJOULES	1831 (436 CAL)
PROTEIN	34 g
FAT	21.4 g
SATURATED FAT	7.4 g
CARBOHYDRATE	24.2 g
FIBRE	6.6 g

Preheat the oven to 170°C (325°F/Gas 3). Toss the sweet potato in a baking dish with 1 teaspoon of the olive oil. Roast for 25 minutes, or until tender.

Meanwhile, heat the remaining olive oil in a large frying pan. Add the leek, onion, garlic and half the basil and sauté over medium–low heat for 10 minutes, or until the onion is cooked and softened. Add the spinach, then cover and cook until just wilted (you may need to wilt the spinach in batches). Remove the pan from the heat and allow the spinach to cool, then drain off any excess liquid.

Whisk the yoghurt with the eggs and season with freshly ground black pepper.

Line a 23 cm (9 inch) square baking dish with baking paper. Arrange the roasted sweet potato in the dish, then spread the spinach mixture over the top. Scatter with the pine nuts, feta, remaining basil and parmesan. Pour the egg mixture over the top and use a fork to pierce holes in the surface so the liquid can spread through to the bottom.

Bake for 35–40 minutes, or until the frittata is puffed and golden and the egg has set. Serve hot or cold.

- 400 g (14 oz) sweet potato, peeled and cut into 3 cm (1^1/$_4$ inch) cubes
- 2 teaspoons olive oil
- 2 leeks, white part only, cut in quarters lengthways, then washed and sliced
- 1 red onion, roughly chopped
- 3 garlic cloves, crushed
- a small handful of basil
- 400 g (14 oz) baby English spinach leaves
- 400 g (14 oz) fat-free plain yoghurt
- 8 eggs
- 2 teaspoons pine nuts
- 50 g (1^3/$_4$ oz) reduced-fat feta cheese, crumbled
- 40 g (1^1/$_2$ oz/^{1}/$_3$ cup) shaved parmesan cheese

serving tip Serve with warm Italian-style bread and a green salad. Delicious with caramelized onions (see page 143) or chilli relish (see page 183)

nutrition tip Excellent source of vitamin C and iron (non-haem)

teriyaki beef with cucumber salad

Serves 4

PER SERVE	
KILOJOULES	944 (225 CAL)
PROTEIN	33 g
FAT	7.7 g
SATURATED FAT	3.2 g
CARBOHYDRATE	3.4 g
FIBRE	0.8 g

- 4 x 150 g (5^1/$_2$ oz) scotch fillet steaks, trimmed of fat
- 60 ml (2 fl oz/^{1}/$_4$ cup) salt-reduced soy sauce
- 2 tablespoons mirin
- 1 tablespoon sake (optional)
- 1 garlic clove, crushed
- 1 teaspoon grated fresh ginger
- olive oil spray
- 1 teaspoon sesame seeds, toasted

CUCUMBER SALAD

- 1 large Lebanese (short) cucumber, peeled, seeded and diced
- ^{1}/$_2$ red capsicum (pepper), diced
- 2 spring onions (scallions), sliced thinly on the diagonal
- 1 teaspoon sugar
- 1 tablespoon rice vinegar

Lay the steaks in a non-metallic dish. Mix together the soy sauce, mirin, sake (if using), garlic and ginger and pour over the steaks. Cover and refrigerate for at least 30 minutes.

Meanwhile, make the cucumber salad. Put the cucumber, capsicum and spring onion in a small bowl. Place the sugar, vinegar and 60 ml (2 fl oz/^{1}/$_4$ cup) water in a small saucepan and stir over medium heat until the sugar has dissolved. Increase the heat and simmer rapidly for 3–4 minutes, or until slightly thickened. Pour over the cucumber salad, stir to combine and leave to cool completely.

Spray a chargrill pan or barbecue plate with olive oil spray and heat until very hot. Drain the steaks and reserve the marinade. Cook the steaks for 3–4 minutes on each side, or until done to your liking. Set aside on a plate, cover loosely with foil and allow to rest for 5–10 minutes before slicing.

Meanwhile, pour the reserved marinade into a small saucepan and bring to the boil. Reduce the heat and simmer for 2–3 minutes, then remove from the heat and keep warm.

Carefully slice each steak into strips 1 cm (^{1}/$_2$ inch) thick and arrange on four plates. Drizzle with the marinade and sprinkle with the sesame seeds. Serve with the cucumber salad.

serving tip Serve with cold soba noodles or steamed basmati rice

nutrition tip Excellent source of vitamin C, zinc and iron

asian-style steamed fish

Serves 4

PER SERVE	
KILOJOULES	953 (227 CAL)
PROTEIN	35 g
FAT	9.2 g
SATURATED FAT	2 g
CARBOHYDRATE	0.7 g
FIBRE	0.4 g

Put the fish fillets in a large frying pan and add enough water to reach halfway up the side of the fish. Cover the pan, bring to a gentle boil and simmer for 3–4 minutes, or until the fish is just cooked through.

Lift out the fish fillets using a slotted spatula and place on four warm plates. Sprinkle with the spring onion and ginger and drizzle with the soy sauce.

Meanwhile, heat the olive oil in a small saucepan, then slowly drizzle the warm oil over each fish fillet. Garnish with coriander leaves.

- 4 x 150 g (5½ oz) fish fillets, such as ocean perch
- 3 spring onions (scallions), finely sliced
- 1 tablespoon finely shredded fresh ginger
- 1 tablespoon salt-reduced soy sauce
- 1 tablespoon olive oil
- a small handful of coriander (cilantro) leaves

serving tip Serve with garlic vegetables (see page 136) and steamed jasmine rice

chargrilled vegetable pasta salad

Serves 4

PER SERVE	
KILOJOULES	2418 (576 CAL)
PROTEIN	23.1 g
FAT	9.6 g
SATURATED FAT	2.4 g
CARBOHYDRATE	93 g
FIBRE	10.2 g

- 150 g (5^1/2 oz) chargrilled eggplant (aubergine)
- 150 g (5^1/2 oz) chargrilled red capsicum (pepper)
- 150 g (5^1/2 oz) chargrilled mushrooms
- 100 g (3^1/2 oz) chargrilled zucchini (courgette)
- 150 g (5^1/2 oz/^{3}/4 cup) sliced chargrilled artichokes
- 4 tablespoons chopped oil-free semi-dried (sun-blushed) tomatoes
- 70 g (2^1/2 oz/2 cups) rocket (arugula) leaves
- 1 tablespoon fresh oregano, or 1 teaspoon dried
- 500 g (1 lb 2 oz) penne pasta
- 60 g (2^1/4 oz) reduced-fat feta cheese

DRESSING
- 1 tablespoon olive oil
- 2 tablespoons white wine vinegar
- 2 teaspoons balsamic vinegar
- 1 garlic clove, crushed

Cut all the chargrilled vegetables into bite-sized pieces and place in a large salad bowl. Add the tomato, rocket, oregano and some freshly ground black pepper.

Put the dressing ingredients in a screw-top jar with some freshly ground black pepper and shake well to combine.

Bring a large saucepan of water to the boil and cook the pasta according to the packet instructions until *al dente*. Drain, briefly rinse with cold water, then drain again. Toss the warm pasta through the vegetable mixture with the dressing. Crumble the feta over the top and serve.

cook's tip Chargrilled vegetables and oil-free semi-dried tomatoes are sold in delicatessens and most large supermarkets

nutrition tip Excellent source of vitamin C. One serve contains one-third of the daily adequate intake of dietary fibre

seafood risotto

Serves 4

PER SERVE	
KILOJOULES	1737 (414 CAL)
PROTEIN	33.5 g
FAT	4.7 g
SATURATED FAT	1 g
CARBOHYDRATE	57 g
FIBRE	2.2 g

Pour the stock into a small saucepan and add the paprika. Bring just to the boil, then reduce the heat and keep at a low simmer.

Heat 1 teaspoon of the olive oil in a heavy-based saucepan, then add the tomato, onion and garlic. Reduce the heat to low and sauté for 5–6 minutes, or until the onion is soft and translucent. Add the rice and stir for 1 minute, or until all the grains are coated.

Increase the heat to medium and begin adding the simmering stock, a ladleful at a time, stirring constantly with a wooden spoon until absorbed. Keep stirring the rice and ladling in the stock until all the stock is absorbed and the grains are tender — this should take about 20 minutes.

Meanwhile, heat the remaining olive oil in a non-stick frying pan over medium–high heat. Add the prawns and cook until they just turn pink. Remove and set aside, then cook the fish pieces, scallops and squid in batches for 1–2 minutes, or until lightly golden. Remove and set aside with the prawns.

When the rice is cooked, stir the seafood and parsley through. Season to taste with freshly ground black pepper and serve immediately with lemon wedges.

- 1.125 litres (40 fl oz/ 4½ cups) salt-reduced fish or chicken stock
- ½ teaspoon paprika
- 2 teaspoons olive oil
- 2 tomatoes, chopped
- 1 onion, finely chopped
- 2 garlic cloves, crushed
- 275 g (9¾ oz/1¼ cups) risotto rice
- 8 small raw prawns (shrimp), peeled and deveined, tails intact
- 200 g (7 oz) firm white fish fillet, bones removed, cut into 4 cm (1¼ inch) pieces
- 8 small scallops, with coral
- 3 small squid tubes, cleaned and cut into rings
- 2 tablespoons chopped flat-leaf (Italian) parsley
- lemon wedges, to serve

serving tip Serve with a rocket salad (see page 124)

nutrition tip Excellent source of vitamin C, and a good source of zinc and omega-3 fat

chicken and noodles with honey lime dressing

Serves 4

PER SERVE	
KILOJOULES	1860 (443 CAL)
PROTEIN	39.5 g
FAT	9.2 g
SATURATED FAT	2.6 g
CARBOHYDRATE	48 g
FIBRE	3.8 g

- 600 g (1 lb 5 oz) boneless, skinless chicken breasts, trimmed of fat
- 400 g (14 oz) thin egg noodles
- 150 g (5^1/$_2$ oz/1^1/$_2$ cups) snow peas (mangetout), trimmed and cut in half on the diagonal
- 180 g (6^1/$_2$ oz/2 cups) bean sprouts, trimmed
- 2 celery stalks, julienned
- 2 large handfuls of mint

HONEY LIME DRESSING
- 1 tablespoon honey
- 3 tablespoons light salt-reduced soy sauce
- grated zest and juice of 1 lime
- 2 red Asian shallots, or French shallots, finely chopped
- 1 teaspoon grated fresh ginger
- 1 small red chilli, seeded and finely chopped

Put the chicken breasts in a saucepan, add enough water to cover, then gently poach for 10 minutes, or until well cooked. Drain, allow to cool, then shred the chicken.

Meanwhile, combine the honey lime dressing ingredients in a small bowl.

Put the noodles in a heatproof bowl, cover with boiling water and leave for 1 minute to soften. Drain, then refresh under cold running water. Cut the noodles into short lengths using kitchen scissors and place in a large serving bowl.

Blanch the snow peas in a saucepan of boiling water for 1 minute, then drain and refresh under cold running water. Add to the noodles with the chicken, dressing and remaining ingredients and toss well to combine.

cook's tip Substitute pork or prawns (shrimp) for the chicken. Also, you can use any thin noodles for this dish — simply cook them according to the packet instructions

nutrition tip Excellent source of vitamin C

chilli calamari with asian salad

Serves 4

PER SERVE	
KILOJOULES	1820 (433 CAL)
PROTEIN	37 g
FAT	5.4 g
SATURATED FAT	1.1 g
CARBOHYDRATE	56 g
FIBRE	5 g

Combine the marinade ingredients in a large, non-metallic bowl. Lightly score the skin of the squid in a zigzag pattern. Slice the squid into 5 cm (2 inch) pieces and add them to the marinade, tossing until well coated. Cover and refrigerate for 30 minutes, or longer if possible.

Meanwhile, cook the noodles in a large saucepan of boiling water for 10 minutes, or according to the packet instructions. Drain, then rinse well in cold water and drain again. Cut the noodles into shorter lengths using kitchen scissors, then place in a salad bowl. Add the capsicum, shallot, salad leaves and bean sprouts.

In a small bowl, mix together the lemon dressing ingredients and set aside.

Lightly spray a barbecue flat plate or large frying pan with olive oil spray and heat until very hot. Drain the squid from the marinade and cook, tossing frequently, for 2 minutes, or until just tender.

Toss the squid through the salad with the lemon dressing. Serve immediately.

MARINADE
- grated zest and juice of 1 lemon
- 2 tablespoons ready-made sweet chilli sauce
- 1 teaspoon canola oil

- 8 large cleaned squid tubes
- 270 g (9 1/2 oz) packet of dried udon noodles
- 1 small red capsicum (pepper), thinly sliced
- 3 red Asian shallots, or French shallots, thinly sliced
- 200 g (7 oz) baby Asian salad leaves
- 180 g (6 oz/2 cups) bean sprouts, trimmed
- olive oil spray

LEMON DRESSING
- 2 tablespoons lemon juice
- 2 tablespoons rice vinegar
- 2 teaspoons grated palm sugar (jaggery) or soft brown sugar
- 1 tablespoon salt-reduced fish sauce
- 1 small red chilli, seeded and chopped

cook's tip Instead of the calamari you could use prawns (shrimp), or thick, firm white fish fillets

nutrition tip An excellent source of vitamin C, and a good source of iron and zinc

stir-fried beef and noodles

Serves 4

PER SERVE	
KILOJOULES	2597 (618 CAL)
PROTEIN	47.2 g
FAT	13.6 g
SATURATED FAT	4.1 g
CARBOHYDRATE	72 g
FIBRE	6.8 g

- 400 g (14 oz) packet of fresh rice noodles
- olive oil spray
- 2 eggs, lightly beaten
- 2 teaspoons peanut oil
- 500 g (1 lb 2 oz) lean rump steak, trimmed and thinly sliced across the grain
- 3 tablespoons kecap manis*
- 1 1/2 tablespoons salt-reduced soy sauce
- 1 1/2 tablespoons salt-reduced fish sauce
- 300 g (10 1/2 oz) Chinese broccoli (gai larn), cut into 5 cm (2 inch) lengths
- 1/4 teaspoon ground white pepper
- lemon wedges, to serve

Put the noodles in a large heatproof bowl, cover with boiling water and soak for 8 minutes, or until softened (or follow the packet instructions). Gently separate the noodles and drain.

Heat a wok over medium heat and spray with olive oil spray. Add the beaten eggs, swirl to coat and cook for 1–2 minutes, or until set into an omelette. Slide the omelette onto a chopping board, roll it up and cut into shreds.

Reheat the wok over high heat, add the peanut oil and swirl to coat. Stir-fry the beef in batches for 3 minutes, or until browned. Remove from the wok and set aside.

Reduce the heat to medium, add the noodles and stir-fry for 2 minutes. Combine the kecap manis, soy sauce and fish sauce, then add to the wok with the broccoli and white pepper. Stir-fry for a further 2 minutes. Return the egg and beef to the wok and stir-fry for another 3 minutes, or until the broccoli has wilted and the noodles are soft but not falling apart. Serve with lemon wedges.

* Kecap manis is an Indonesian sauce similar to a sweet-tasting soy sauce. It is available from most supermarkets and Asian food stores.

nutrition tip Excellent source of vitamin C, iron and zinc

cook's tip For extra crunch and nutrients, add 100 g (3 1/2 oz/1 cup) finely sliced snow peas (mangetout) to the wok with the broccoli

chargrilled tuna with ruby grapefruit salad

Serves 4

PER SERVE	
KILOJOULES	1405 (335 CAL)
PROTEIN	40.3 g
FAT	14.8 g
SATURATED FAT	4.3 g
CARBOHYDRATE	9.2 g
FIBRE	1.8 g

Cut a slice off each end of the grapefruit and peel away the skin, removing all the pith. Separate the segments and set aside in a bowl.

Put all the mint dressing ingredients in a small screw-top jar and shake until well combined.

Lightly spray a chargrill pan or barbecue hotplate with olive oil spray and heat until very hot. Cook the tuna steaks for 3–4 minutes on each side, so the centre is still slightly pink (overcooking the tuna will make the flesh tough).

Divide the rocket among four plates and top with the grapefruit segments and onion. Drizzle with the dressing and serve with the tuna steaks and lime wedges.

- 4 ruby grapefruit
- olive oil spray
- 4 x 150 g (5^1/$_2$ oz) tuna steaks
- 150 g (5^1/$_2$ oz) rocket (arugula) leaves
- 1 small red onion, thinly sliced
- lime wedges, to serve

MINT DRESSING
- 1 tablespoon olive oil
- 1^1/$_2$ tablespoons red wine vinegar
- 1 tablespoon shredded mint

serving tip Serve with crusty sourdough bread and tzatziki (see page 55)

nutrition tip An excellent source of vitamin C, and a good source of iron and omega-3 fat

fresh vegetable lasagne with rocket

Serves 4

PER SERVE	
KILOJOULES	1874 (446 CAL)
PROTEIN	22.2 g
FAT	13.5 g
SATURATED FAT	4.5 g
CARBOHYDRATE	51.3 g
FIBRE	15.4 g

- 150 g (5^1/$_2$ oz/1 cup) fresh or frozen peas
- 16 asparagus spears, trimmed and cut into 5 cm (2 inch) lengths
- 2 large zucchini (courgettes), cut into thin ribbons
- 100 g (3^1/$_2$ oz) rocket (arugula) leaves
- a very large handful of basil, torn
- 1 tablespoon olive oil
- 2 fresh lasagne sheets (200 g/7 oz in total), each about 24 x 35 cm (9^1/$_2$ x 14 inches)
- 150 g (5^1/$_2$ oz/1 cup) chopped fat-free semi-dried (sun-blushed) tomatoes
- 250 g (9 oz/1 cup) low-fat ricotta cheese
- 1 tablespoon balsamic vinegar
- shaved parmesan cheese, to serve

Bring a large saucepan of water to the boil. Blanch the peas, asparagus and zucchini in separate batches until just tender, removing each batch with a slotted spoon and refreshing under cold running water (reserve the cooking liquid). Toss the vegetables in a mixing bowl with the rocket, basil, olive oil and some freshly ground black pepper.

Return the cooking liquid to the boil and cook the lasagne sheets for 1–2 minutes, or until *al dente*. Refresh in cold water, drain well, then cut each sheet in half lengthways.

To assemble, place one strip of pasta on a serving plate so it overhangs on both sides. Place a small amount of the salad down the centre, then some tomato and ricotta. Season lightly and fold over one-third of the lasagne sheet. Top with another layer of salad, tomato and ricotta. Fold the final layer of pasta over and garnish with a little salad and tomato.

Repeat with the remaining pasta, salad, tomato and ricotta to make four individual servings. Serve drizzled with the balsamic vinegar and scattered with shaved parmesan.

serving tip Serve with caramelized onions (see page 143)

nutrition tip Excellent source of vitamin C, a good source of calcium and high in fibre

vegetarian paella

Serves 6

PER SERVE	
KILOJOULES	1495 (356 CAL)
PROTEIN	15.6 g
FAT	6.7 g
SATURATED FAT	1 g
CARBOHYDRATE	52.3 g
FIBRE	11.2 g

Heat the olive oil in a large paella pan or frying pan. Add the onion and capsicum and sauté over medium–high heat for 5 minutes, or until the onion has softened. Stir in the garlic and cook for 1 minute.

Add the rice, paprika and mixed spice and stir to coat. Stir in the stock, tomato and tomato paste and bring to the boil. Cover, reduce the heat and simmer for 20 minutes.

Meanwhile, cut the stems from the silverbeet, rinse the leaves and finely shred them. Put the cannellini beans, soya beans, silverbeet and artichoke on top of the rice, then cover the pan and cook for 10 minutes, or until all the liquid is absorbed and the rice is tender. Turn off the heat, stir the beans and vegetables through and leave for 5 minutes. Stir in the coriander and serve with lemon wedges.

- 1 tablespoon olive oil
- 1 onion, diced
- 1 red capsicum (pepper), cut into 1 x 4 cm ($1/2$ x $1^1/2$ inch) strips
- 5 garlic cloves, crushed
- 275 g ($9^3/4$ oz/$1^1/4$ cups) paella rice or arborio rice
- 2 teaspoons sweet paprika
- $1/2$ teaspoon mixed (pumpkin pie) spice
- 750 ml (26 fl oz/3 cups) salt-reduced vegetable stock
- 400 g (14 oz) tin no-added-salt chopped tomatoes
- $1^1/2$ tablespoons no-added-salt tomato paste (concentrated purée)
- 400 g (14 oz/1 bunch) silverbeet (Swiss chard)
- 400 g (14 oz) tin cannellini beans, rinsed and drained
- 300 g ($10^1/2$ oz) tin soya beans, rinsed and drained
- 280 g (10 oz) jar fat-free artichoke hearts, drained and cut into quarters
- 4 tablespoons chopped coriander (cilantro) leaves
- lemon wedges, to serve

nutrition tip Excellent source of vitamin C

cook's tip For a seafood paella, omit the beans and top with cooked prawns (shrimp) and calamari rings

poached salmon with mango salsa

Serves 4

PER SERVE	
KILOJOULES	1722 (410 CAL)
PROTEIN	40.7 g
FAT	23.5 g
SATURATED FAT	5 g
CARBOHYDRATE	8.5 g
FIBRE	2 g

MANGO SALSA
- 1 ripe mango, flesh cubed
- 1/2 ripe avocado, flesh cubed
- 1/2 red onion, finely chopped
- 2–3 tablespoons finely sliced basil
- juice of 1 lime
- 2 teaspoons olive oil

- 4 x 200 g (7 oz) salmon fillets, pin bones removed
- 1 bay leaf
- a few black peppercorns
- 1/2 red onion, roughly chopped
- 1 teaspoon white wine vinegar

Put all the mango salsa ingredients in a small bowl. Gently stir together, then cover and set aside.

Put the salmon fillets in a large frying pan and add enough water to reach halfway up the side of the fish. Add the bay leaf, peppercorns, onion and vinegar. Cover, bring to a gentle boil and simmer for 10 minutes, or until cooked to your liking.

Lift out the salmon using a slotted spatula, drain well and place on four warm plates. Top with the mango salsa and serve.

nutrition tip Excellent source of vitamin C, and a good source of omega-3 fat

serving tip Serve with garlic vegetables (see page 136) and boiled new potatoes, steamed rice or vermicelli noodles

home-style lentil soup

Serves 4

PER SERVE	
KILOJOULES	1433 (341 CAL)
PROTEIN	25.6 g
FAT	2.2 g
SATURATED FAT	0.3 g
CARBOHYDRATE	45.8 g
FIBRE	17.2 g

Put the lentils in a large saucepan and cover with water. Bring to the boil, then drain immediately into a colander.

Return the lentils to the saucepan. Add 2 litres (70 fl oz/8 cups) water and all the other ingredients except the parsley. Bring to the boil, then reduce the heat, cover and simmer for 1^1/$_2$ hours, stirring occasionally, and adding extra water if needed. Season to taste with freshly ground black pepper — if the soup is very thick, thin it with a little water. Serve sprinkled with the parsley.

- 370 g (13 oz/2 cups) brown lentils
- 1 capsicum (pepper), finely chopped
- 1 carrot, finely chopped
- 1 onion, finely chopped
- 3 garlic cloves, finely chopped
- 250 ml (9 fl oz/1 cup) salt-reduced tomato paste (concentrated purée)
- 1 chicken stock (bouillon) cube
- 1 bay leaf
- ^{1}/$_4$ teaspoon ground cumin
- ^{1}/$_4$ teaspoon ground coriander
- a pinch of paprika
- 3 tablespoons chopped parsley

serving tip Serve with warm wholegrain or toasted Italian-style bread

nutrition tip Excellent source of vitamin C and iron (non-haem). One serve contains over half the adequate daily intake of dietary fibre

chicken a l'orange

Serves 4

PER SERVE	
KILOJOULES	1394 (332 CAL)
PROTEIN	38.9 g
FAT	15.7 g
SATURATED FAT	3.5 g
CARBOHYDRATE	8.2 g
FIBRE	1.5 g

ORANGE AND REDCURRANT SAUCE

- 2 teaspoons finely grated orange zest
- 125 ml (4 fl oz/^{1}/$_2$ cup) fresh orange juice
- 60 ml (2 fl oz/^{1}/$_4$ cup) salt-reduced chicken stock
- 2 teaspoons redcurrant jelly

- wholemeal (whole-wheat) flour, for dusting
- 4 x 150 g (5^1/$_2$ oz) boneless, skinless chicken breasts
- 2 teaspoons olive oil
- 2 teaspoons cornflour
- 1 tablespoon finely chopped parsley
- 1 tablespoon flaked almonds, toasted

Preheat the oven to 190°C (375°F/Gas 5). Put the orange and redcurrant sauce ingredients in a small saucepan and stir over medium heat for 1 minute, or until the redcurrant jelly has dissolved. Set aside.

Season the flour with some cracked black pepper and use it to lightly dust the chicken breasts.

Heat the olive oil in a large frying pan over medium heat and lightly brown the chicken for 1 minute on each side.

Transfer the chicken to a baking dish and pour the orange and redcurrant sauce over the top. Bake for 20 minutes, or until the chicken is cooked through.

Mix the cornflour to a smooth paste with 2 teaspoons water. Spoon the orange and redcurrant sauce from the baking dish back into the same saucepan it was warmed in, then add the cornflour paste and stir for 2–3 minutes, or until the sauce has thickened. Arrange the chicken breasts on four warm plates, drizzle with the sauce and sprinkle with the parsley and flaked almonds.

serving tip Serve with snow peas and poppy seeds (see page 131) and steamed long-grain brown rice

tagliatelle with smoked salmon and asparagus

Serves 4

PER SERVE	
KILOJOULES	2183 (520 CAL)
PROTEIN	30.2 g
FAT	9.6 g
SATURATED FAT	2 g
CARBOHYDRATE	72.7 g
DIETARY FIBRE	9.8 g

Bring a large saucepan of water to the boil and cook the tagliatelle according to the packet instructions until *al dente*. Drain well.

Put the leek and half the stock in a large, deep frying pan. Cook over low heat, stirring often, for 4–5 minutes. Stir in the garlic, peas and mint and cook for 1 minute. Add the remaining stock and 125 ml (4 fl oz/^{1}/$_2$ cup) water and bring to the boil, then reduce the heat and simmer for 5 minutes.

Stir in the asparagus, parsley and basil and simmer for a further 3–4 minutes, or until the asparagus is just tender. If necessary, gradually increase the heat to reduce the sauce to a light coating consistency. Stir in the nutmeg, parmesan and smoked salmon and add a good grind of black pepper.

Add the pasta to the sauce and toss lightly to coat. Serve drizzled with the olive oil, and scattered with a little extra grated parmesan and chopped parsley or basil.

nutrition tip Excellent source of vitamin C, and a good source of iron and omega-3 fat

- 375 g (13 oz) dried or 500 g (1 lb 2 oz) fresh tagliatelle
- 2 leeks, white part only, rinsed and finely sliced
- 250 ml (9 fl oz/1 cup) salt-reduced chicken or vegetable stock
- 3 garlic cloves, crushed
- 235 g (8^1/$_2$ oz/1^1/$_2$ cups) shelled fresh peas
- 1 tablespoon finely chopped mint
- 400 g (14 oz/2 large bunches) asparagus, trimmed and cut into 5 cm (2 inch) lengths
- 3 tablespoons finely chopped parsley, plus extra to serve (optional)
- a very large handful of basil, shredded, plus extra to serve (optional)
- a pinch of nutmeg
- 2 tablespoons grated parmesan cheese, plus extra to serve (optional)
- 200 g (7 oz) smoked salmon, cut into strips
- 1 tablespoon olive oil

serving tip Serve with a tomato basil salad (see page 128)

simple chicken casserole

Serves 4

PER SERVE	
KILOJOULES	1807 (430 CAL)
PROTEIN	49.8 g
FAT	18.7 g
SATURATED FAT	5.6 g
CARBOHYDRATE	14.5 g
FIBRE	3.5 g

- 6 boneless, skinless chicken thighs, trimmed of all fat
- 3 carrots, chopped
- 1 red capsicum (pepper), roughly chopped
- 1 red onion, roughly chopped
- 400 g (14 oz) tin chopped tomatoes
- 4 tablespoons white vinegar
- 2 tablespoons soft brown sugar
- 2 tablespoons chopped parsley, plus extra, to serve
- 2 teaspoons dijon mustard
- 2 teaspoons salt-reduced soy sauce

Preheat the oven to 180°C (350°F/Gas 4). Put the chicken in a baking dish and scatter the vegetables over the top. Combine the remaining ingredients in a large bowl and carefully pour over the chicken.

Bake, uncovered, for 1 1/4 hours, or until the chicken is cooked through and the vegetables are soft. Serve sprinkled with some extra parsley.

nutrition tip Excellent source of vitamin C and zinc, and a good source of iron

serving tip Serve with steamed long-grain brown rice and zesty greens (see page 139)

moroccan lamb

Serves 4

PER SERVE	
KILOJOULES	2022 (481 CAL)
PROTEIN	49.4 g
FAT	14.1 g
SATURATED FAT	5 g
CARBOHYDRATE	33.2 g
FIBRE	12.1 g

Heat the olive oil in a large saucepan over high heat and brown the lamb in batches for 2–3 minutes. Reduce the heat to medium, then return all the lamb to the pan with the onion and garlic and sauté for 5 minutes. Add the ground spices, season with freshly ground black pepper and cook for 2 minutes. Stir in the coriander, tomato, stock and 500 ml (17 fl oz/2 cups) water and bring to the boil over high heat.

Add the lentils, then reduce the heat to low. Cover and simmer for 1 1/2 hours. Stir in the chickpeas and simmer, uncovered, for a further 30 minutes, or until the lamb is tender and the sauce is thick. Season with freshly ground black pepper and serve scattered with coriander leaves.

- 2 teaspoons olive oil
- 600 g (1 lb 5 oz) boned leg of lamb, cut into 1 cm (1/2 inch) cubes
- 1 onion, chopped
- 2 garlic cloves, crushed
- 1/2 teaspoon ground cinnamon
- 1/2 teaspoon ground turmeric
- 1/2 teaspoon ground ginger
- 4 tablespoons chopped coriander (cilantro)
- 2 x 400 g (14 oz) tins no-added-salt chopped tomatoes
- 1 litre (35 fl oz/4 cups) salt-reduced chicken stock
- 160 g (5 1/2 oz/2/3 cup) dried red lentils, rinsed
- 300 g (10 1/2 oz) tin chickpeas, rinsed and drained
- coriander (cilantro) leaves, to serve

serving tip Serve with steamed couscous

nutrition tip Excellent source of vitamin C, iron and zinc

madras beef curry

Serves 6

PER SERVE	
KILOJOULES	1540 (367 CAL)
PROTEIN	39.4 g
FAT	15.9 g
SATURATED FAT	4.4 g
CARBOHYDRATE	14.4 g
FIBRE	5 g

- 1 tablespoon vegetable oil
- 2 onions, finely chopped
- 3 garlic cloves, finely chopped
- 1 tablespoon grated fresh ginger
- 4 tablespoons madras curry paste
- 1 kg (2 lb 4 oz) chuck steak, trimmed of fat and cut into 3 cm (1 1/4 inch) cubes
- 3 tablespoons no-added-salt tomato paste (concentrated purée)
- 250 ml (9 fl oz/1 cup) salt-reduced beef stock
- 6 small new potatoes, cut in half
- 150 g (5 1/2 oz/1 cup) frozen peas
- coriander (cilantro) sprigs, to serve

Preheat the oven to 180°C (350°F/Gas 4). Heat the vegetable oil in a heavy-based 3 litre (105 fl oz/12 cup) flameproof casserole dish. Add the onion and sauté over medium heat for 4–5 minutes. Add the garlic and ginger and sauté for a further 5 minutes, or until the onion is lightly golden, taking care not to let it burn.

Add the curry paste and sauté for 2 minutes, or until fragrant. Increase the heat to high, add the beef and stir constantly for 2–3 minutes, or until the beef is well coated. Stir in the tomato paste and stock.

Cover and bake for 50 minutes, stirring two or three times during cooking, and adding a little water if necessary.

Reduce the oven temperature to 160°C (315°F/Gas 2–3). Add the potato and cook for 30 minutes, then add the peas and cook for another 10 minutes, or until the potato is tender. Serve garnished with coriander sprigs.

serving tip Serve with steamed basmati rice

nutrition tip Excellent source of vitamin C, iron and zinc

beef involtini

Serves 4

PER SERVE	
KILOJOULES	1774 (422 CAL)
PROTEIN	43 g
FAT	11.7 g
SATURATED FAT	4.9 g
CARBOHYDRATE	28 g
FIBRE	6.6 g

Heat a deep, heavy-based frying pan and spray with olive oil spray. Sauté the onion and celery over medium heat for 3 minutes, or until softened. Add the wine and cook until the wine is reduced by two-thirds. Stir in the tomato, tomato paste, thyme sprigs and 500 ml (17 fl oz/2 cups) water. Reduce the heat and simmer, stirring occasionally, for 30 minutes, or until the sauce is thickened and reduced. Remove the thyme sprigs.

Meanwhile, combine all the parsley stuffing ingredients in a bowl. Flatten the steaks with a meat mallet to an even 5 mm (1/4 inch) thickness, then pat dry with paper towels. Divide the parsley stuffing evenly over the steaks. Roll each one up firmly and secure with a toothpick.

Spray a large, non-stick frying pan with olive oil spray and place over medium–high heat. Add the beef rolls and brown them all over, then add to the tomato sauce in a single layer. Bring to the boil, then reduce the heat, cover and simmer for 45 minutes, or until tender, turning the rolls once or twice.

Meanwhile, cook the sweet potato in a saucepan of boiling water for 15 minutes, or until tender. Drain, then pour the milk over and roughly chop using a flat-sided dinner knife.

Serve two beef rolls per person and spoon the sauce over. Top with shredded herbs and serve with the sweet potato mash.

- olive oil spray
- 1 onion, finely chopped
- 1 celery stalk, finely chopped
- 125 ml (4 fl oz/1/2 cup) red wine
- 2 x 400 g (14 oz) tins no-added-salt chopped tomatoes
- 2 tablespoons no-added-salt tomato paste (concentrated pureé)
- 2 thyme sprigs
- 8 x 85 g (3 oz) minute steaks
- 500 g (1 lb 2 oz) sweet potato, peeled and cut into 5 cm (2 inch) chunks
- 3 tablespoons skim milk
- shredded herbs, to serve

PARSLEY STUFFING
- a large handful of flat-leaf (Italian) parsley, chopped
- 3 tablespoons grated parmesan cheese
- 3 garlic cloves, finely chopped
- grated zest of 2 large lemons

serving tip Serve with a mixed salad

nutrition tip Excellent source of vitamin C, iron and zinc

herb-crusted lamb roast with vegetables

Serves 4

PER SERVE	
KILOJOULES	1687 (402 CAL)
PROTEIN	40.2 g
FAT	12.2 g
SATURATED FAT	5 g
CARBOHYDRATE	27.4 g
FIBRE	10.6 g

- 6 large carrots, cut into 2 cm ($^3/4$ inch) pieces on the diagonal
- olive oil spray
- 2 tablespoons dijon mustard
- 2 tablespoons finely chopped flat-leaf (Italian) parsley
- 1 teaspoon finely chopped thyme
- 1 teaspoon finely chopped sage
- 3 garlic cloves, crushed
- 2 x 300 g ($10^1/2$ oz) pieces of lamb rump or mini lamb roasts, trimmed of fat
- 400 g (14 oz) baby new potatoes
- 150 g ($5^1/2$ oz) green beans, trimmed and sliced
- 150 g ($5^1/2$ oz/$1^1/2$ cups) snow peas (mangetout), trimmed and sliced
- 135 g ($4^3/4$ oz/1 cup) frozen peas
- 1 mint sprig

Preheat the oven to 200°C (400°F/Gas 6). Spray the carrots with olive oil spray, season with freshly cracked pepper and place in a roasting tin large enough to hold all the lamb pieces as well. Roast the carrots for 30 minutes.

In a bowl, mix together the mustard, herbs and garlic. Add the lamb pieces and turn them about to thoroughly coat with the herbs. Add them to the roasting tin with the carrots and roast for 30 minutes, or until the carrots are golden and soft and the lamb is cooked.

Meanwhile, cook the potatoes in a large saucepan of boiling water for 12 minutes, or until tender. Drain.

Remove the lamb from the oven and place on a board. Cover loosely with foil and allow to rest for 5 minutes.

While the lamb is resting, steam or microwave the beans and snow peas for 2–3 minutes. Cook the frozen peas with the mint sprig in boiling water for 2–3 minutes, then drain.

Carve the lamb across the grain and serve with the potatoes and vegetables.

cook's tip Serve the roast lamb with a Greek salad (see page 127) instead of steamed greens, or with hasselback potatoes (see page 140) instead of baby new potatoes

nutrition tip Excellent source of vitamin C, iron and zinc

peppered beef on potato mash

Serves 4

PER SERVE	
KILOJOULES	1696 (404 CAL)
PROTEIN	46.2 g
FAT	9.8 g
SATURATED FAT	3.6 g
CARBOHYDRATE	26.7 g
FIBRE	11.8 g

Preheat the oven to 180°C (350°F/Gas 4). Spray the potatoes with olive oil spray, season with freshly ground black pepper and place on a large baking tray. Trim the ends of the garlic cloves, leaving the skins on, then add to the baking tray and roast for 40 minutes, or until the potato is golden.

Roughly crush the peppercorns in a spice grinder with the thyme (or use a mortar and pestle). Tip them onto a plate, then roll the steaks in the mixture until well coated.

Heat a chargrill pan or frying pan over medium heat. Spray with olive oil spray, add the steaks and cook for 5 minutes on each side for medium–rare, or until done to your liking. Set aside on a plate, cover loosely with foil and allow to rest for 5 minutes.

Meanwhile, steam or microwave the broccoli for 4 minutes, or until tender.

Squeeze the roasted garlic cloves from their skins and mash them. Bring the stock to the boil in a small saucepan, add the roasted potatoes and mashed garlic and roughly crush them together using a fork, until softened but still quite chunky.

Put the spinach in a saucepan over low–medium heat. Cover and cook for 2 minutes, or until the leaves are just beginning to wilt. Remove from the heat and season with black pepper.

Divide the potato mash and broccoli among four warm plates. Top the mash with the spinach, sit the steak on top and drizzle with any resting juices from the meat.

- 6 medium potatoes, peeled and cut into 3 cm (1 1/4 inch) cubes
- olive oil spray
- 6 garlic cloves, unpeeled
- 2 tablespoons whole black peppercorns
- 1/2 teaspoon dried thyme
- 4 x 160 g (5 1/2 oz) lean beef fillet steaks, trimmed of fat
- 500 g (1 lb 2 oz) broccoli, cut into florets
- 4 tablespoons salt-reduced vegetable stock
- 300 g (10 1/2 oz) baby English spinach leaves

nutrition tip Excellent source of vitamin C, iron and zinc

on the side

'Never too much of a good thing!' That's what we think of the mighty vegetable family. Nutritionally they have so much to offer, which is why national recommendations say to include at least five servings each day. You'll find this very easy to achieve with these simple yet scrumptious ways with vegetables.

rocket salad

PER SERVE	
KILOJOULES	253 (60 CAL)
PROTEIN	2.8 g
FAT	3.2 g
SATURATED FAT	0.7 g
CARBOHYDRATE	4.2 g
FIBRE	2.2 g

Serves 4

- 100 g (3½ oz/2 cups) baby rocket (arugula) leaves
- 3 tomatoes, cut into wedges
- 1 small red onion, thinly sliced
- 2 teaspoons olive oil
- 2 teaspoons balsamic vinegar
- 1 tablespoon shaved parmesan cheese

Toss the rocket, tomato and onion together in a salad bowl and add a sprinkling of freshly cracked black pepper to taste. Drizzle with the olive oil and vinegar, scatter the parmesan over the top and serve.

cook's tip Use baby English spinach leaves if rocket is unavailable

nutrition tip Excellent source of vitamin C

greek salad

Serves 4

PER SERVE	
KILOJOULES	390 (93 CAL)
PROTEIN	6.9 g
FAT	2.4 g
SATURATED FAT	1.2 g
CARBOHYDRATE	8.1 g
FIBRE	5.9 g

Toss the lettuce, cucumber, tomato, olives and feta together in a salad bowl. Mix the oregano leaves through the salad, drizzle with the lemon juice and vinegar and serve.

- 1 cos (romaine) lettuce, shredded
- 2 Lebanese (short) cucumbers, sliced
- 4 tomatoes, cut into wedges
- 60 g (2 1/4 oz / 1/3 cup) whole black olives
- 50 g (1 3/4 oz) fat-reduced feta cheese, crumbled
- dried oregano leaves, to taste
- 1 tablespoon lemon juice, or to taste
- 1 tablespoon white wine vinegar, or to taste

cook's tip To turn the salad into a light meal, top with chargrilled chicken breast strips and serve with crusty bread

nutrition tip Excellent source of vitamin C

tomato basil salad

PER SERVE	
KILOJOULES	197 (47 CAL)
PROTEIN	3 g
FAT	0.4 g
SATURATED FAT	0 g
CARBOHYDRATE	6 g
FIBRE	3.8 g

Serves 4

- 6 ripe roma (plum) tomatoes
- 1 red onion, thinly sliced
- 1 garlic clove, crushed
- 2 tablespoons balsamic vinegar
- 2 large handfuls of basil, shredded

Cut the tomatoes into wedges and place in a bowl. Add the remaining ingredients and toss together. Season with freshly ground black pepper and set aside for 10 minutes, then transfer to a shallow serving dish.

serving tip Add bocconcini (fresh baby mozzarella) cheese and serve with crusty Italian bread for a light meal, or serve over strips of chargrilled chicken breast

nutrition tip Excellent source of vitamin C

cook's tip If you find the taste of raw onion too strong, put it in a bowl and cover with boiling water first for 5 minutes, then drain well before adding to the salad

snow peas and poppy seeds

Serves 4

Toast the poppy seeds in a non-stick frying pan over medium heat for 1–2 minutes. Tip into a small bowl and set aside.

Steam the snow peas for 2 minutes, or until bright green but still crisp. Refresh under cold running water, then drain. Toss in a serving bowl with the poppy seeds and olive oil and serve.

PER SERVE	
KILOJOULES	221 (53 CAL)
PROTEIN	2.8 g
FAT	2.5 g
SATURATED FAT	0.3 g
CARBOHYDRATE	3.6 g
FIBRE	2.3 g

- 1 tablespoon poppy seeds
- 300 g (10 1/2 oz) snow peas (mangetout), trimmed
- 1 teaspoon olive oil

nutrition tip Excellent source of vitamin C

asparagus and green beans with toasted almonds

Serves 4

PER SERVE	
KILOJOULES	342 (81 CAL)
PROTEIN	3.1 g
FAT	6.5 g
SATURATED FAT	0.6 g
CARBOHYDRATE	1.7 g
FIBRE	2.2 g

- 150 g (5$\frac{1}{2}$ oz/1 bunch) trimmed young asparagus
- 100 g (3$\frac{1}{2}$ oz) baby green beans
- 2 teaspoons olive oil
- 30 g (1 oz/$\frac{1}{3}$ cup) flaked almonds, toasted

Add the asparagus and beans to a large saucepan of rapidly boiling water. Cook for 1 minute, or until just tender. Drain, refresh under cold running water, then toss in a bowl with the olive oil and flaked almonds. Season well with freshly ground black pepper and serve.

cook's tip Use pine nuts or walnuts instead of almonds

time saver Almonds can be toasted ahead of time and stored in an airtight container for up to 3 weeks

serving tip Serve with roast beef or chicken

honeyed carrots

PER SERVE	
KILOJOULES	310 (74 CAL)
PROTEIN	0.6 g
FAT	3.2 g
SATURATED FAT	0.5 g
CARBOHYDRATE	9.7 g
FIBRE	2.2 g

Serves 4

Steam the carrots for 5–7 minutes, or until bright in colour and tender, but still slightly firm. Remove from the steamer and set aside for 5 minutes to dry out a little. (Alternatively, use a microwave to cook the carrots.)

Put the olive oil and margarine in a saucepan over high heat. When the oil is hot, add the carrots and honey. Sauté for 5 minutes, tossing frequently, until the honey caramelizes and coats the carrots.

Serve hot, sprinkled with parsley.

- 4 large carrots, peeled and julienned or sliced into 1 cm (1/2 inch) rings
- 2 teaspoons olive oil
- 1 teaspoon margarine
- 1 tablespoon honey
- 1 tablespoon chopped parsley

serving tip Wonderful with steamed green vegetables and skinless grilled chicken

garlic vegetables

PER SERVE	
KILOJOULES	209 (50 CAL)
PROTEIN	2.3 g
FAT	2.6 g
SATURATED FAT	0.3 g
CARBOHYDRATE	3.3 g
FIBRE	2.4 g

Serves 4

- 2 teaspoons olive oil
- 3 garlic cloves, finely chopped
- 200 g (7 oz) snow peas (mangetout), trimmed
- 200 g (7 oz/$^1/_2$ large bunch) baby bok choy (pak choy), larger leaves sliced lengthways

Heat the olive oil in a wok over medium–high heat until hot. Add the garlic, then immediately add the greens. Cook, stirring constantly, for 2 minutes, or until the greens are just slightly cooked.

Sprinkle with freshly cracked black pepper to taste and stir for another 30 seconds. Serve immediately.

nutrition tip Excellent source of vitamin C

zesty greens

Serves 4

PER SERVE	
KILOJOULES	191 (45 CAL)
PROTEIN	3.6 g
FAT	2.5 g
SATURATED FAT	0.3 g
CARBOHYDRATE	0.7 g
FIBRE	3.1 g

Steam the vegetables for 3 minutes, or until bright green but still crisp. Refresh under cold running water, then drain.

Place in a serving bowl and drizzle with the lemon juice, olive oil and freshly cracked black pepper. Serve immediately.

- 300 g (10$\frac{1}{2}$ oz/4 cups) of your favourite chopped green vegetables, such as asparagus, broccoli, zucchini (courgette) or snow peas (mangetout)
- 2 tablespoons lemon juice
- 2 teaspoons olive oil

nutrition tip Excellent source of vitamin C

hasselback potatoes

Serves 6

PER SERVE	
KILOJOULES	362 (86 CAL)
PROTEIN	2.5 g
FAT	2 g
SATURATED FAT	0.3 g
CARBOHYDRATE	13.6 g
FIBRE	1.8 g

- olive oil spray
- 6 potatoes (100 g/3¹/₂ oz each), peeled
- 2 teaspoons olive oil margarine, melted
- onion topping or spice topping (see below)

ONION TOPPING
- 1 garlic clove, crushed
- 2 tablespoons diced red onion

SPICE TOPPING
- 1 teaspoon paprika
- ¹/₂ teaspoon ground cumin
- a pinch of cayenne pepper

Preheat the oven to 220°C (425°F/Gas 7). Lightly spray a shallow baking dish with olive oil spray.

Cut a thin slice from the bottom of each potato, then place them cut side down on a work surface. (They should sit flat and not roll when you cut a series of parallel incisions across the back.)

Lay a wooden spoon handle parallel to one side of a potato, then slice the potato thinly, cutting as far as the spoon handle to prevent cutting all the way through. Repeat with the remaining potatoes.

Sit the potatoes in the baking dish and fan the slices out slightly. Brush the tops with the melted margarine, sprinkle with freshly cracked black pepper and bake for 45 minutes.

Combine your chosen topping ingredients in a bowl. Remove the potatoes from the oven and sprinkle the topping over the potatoes. Bake for a further 10 minutes, then serve.

cook's tip Cut the potatoes into slices, drizzle with olive oil and sprinkle with chopped rosemary before baking

caramelized onions

PER SERVE	
KILOJOULES	415 (99 CAL)
PROTEIN	2.1 g
FAT	4.7 g
SATURATED FAT	0.7 g
CARBOHYDRATE	11.1 g
FIBRE	2.1 g

Serves 4

Heat a large saucepan over medium–high heat. Add the olive oil and onions, then cover and cook, stirring frequently, for 15 minutes, or until golden and caramelized.

Add the sugar, vinegar and some cracked black pepper. Stir until the sugar has dissolved, then turn up the heat a little and cook uncovered for 8–10 minutes, stirring occasionally, until the liquid becomes thick and syrupy.

Stir in the mustard, if using, and serve hot or at room temperature. If you're not serving the caramelized onions straight away, transfer to a sterilized 250 ml (9 fl oz/1 cup) jar and refrigerate until needed.

- 1 tablespoon olive oil
- 500 g (1 lb 2 oz) brown onions, thinly sliced
- 1 tablespoon raw (demerara) sugar
- 125 ml (4 fl oz/$\frac{1}{2}$ cup) red wine vinegar
- 1–2 teaspoons wholegrain mustard, to taste (optional)

cook's tip This versatile accompaniment goes well with just about any savoury dish!

storage tip Keeps for up to 3 months in a sterilized jar in the refrigerator

balsamic mushrooms

Serves 4

PER SERVE	
KILOJOULES	178 (42 CAL)
PROTEIN	3.3 g
FAT	2.6 g
SATURATED FAT	0.3 g
CARBOHYDRATE	0.4 g
FIBRE	2.5 g

- 2 teaspoons olive oil
- 350 g (12 oz/about 4 cups) thickly sliced button mushrooms
- 2 garlic cloves, finely chopped
- 2 tablespoons balsamic vinegar
- 1 tablespoon fresh thyme

Heat the olive oil in a non-stick frying pan. Add the mushrooms and garlic and sauté over medium–high heat for 5 minutes, or until the mushrooms are soft.

Increase the heat to high, add the balsamic vinegar and cook for 1–2 minutes, or until the vinegar has evaporated. Stir in the thyme and serve.

cook's tip Delicious with beef, chicken or eggs. Makes a quick and easy light meal or brunch served on a thick slice of sourdough toast

sweet things

Most people believe they must shy away from sweets to manage their weight. But guess what? As long as they're not laden with excess fat and sugar, you can still enjoy sweet treats. Fruit is a wonderful ingredient that offers natural sweetness, as well as essential vitamins and minerals.

fruit salad with ginger lime syrup

Serves 4

PER SERVE	
KILOJOULES	549 (131 CAL)
PROTEIN	2.9 g
FAT	0.6 g
SATURATED FAT	0 g
CARBOHYDRATE	26 g
FIBRE	5.3 g

Cut all the fruit except the strawberries into 3 cm (1¹/4 inch) cubes and place in a large serving bowl. Hull the strawberries, cut them in half and add to the fruit with the mint leaves. Gently mix together.

To make the ginger lime syrup, put the sugar, lime juice and 125 ml (4 fl oz/¹/2 cup) water in a small saucepan. Stir over low heat until the sugar has dissolved. Add the ginger and bring to the boil, then reduce the heat and simmer for 10 minutes, or until reduced to a syrup. Allow to cool slightly, then pour over the fruit salad and refrigerate until cold.

- ¹/2 small ripe pineapple
- 500 g (1 lb 2 oz) seedless watermelon
- 300 g (10¹/2 oz) rockmelon or any orange-fleshed melon
- ¹/2 papaya
- 250 g (9 oz/1²/3 cups) strawberries
- 3 tablespoons small mint leaves

GINGER LIME SYRUP
- 2 tablespoons soft brown sugar
- 125 ml (4 fl oz/¹/2 cup) lime juice
- 2 cm (³/4 inch) knob of fresh ginger, peeled and grated

nutrition tip Excellent source of vitamin C

serving tip Serve with low-fat vanilla yoghurt or ricotta cream (see page 154)

cook's tip Use any seasonal fruit

apricot and apple strudel

Serves 4

PER SERVE	
KILOJOULES	630 (150 CAL)
PROTEIN	3 g
FAT	3.8 g
SATURATED FAT	0.5 g
CARBOHYDRATE	24.3 g
FIBRE	2.9 g

- 60 g (2$\frac{1}{4}$ oz/$\frac{1}{3}$ cup) dried apricots
- 1 small granny smith apple, peeled, cored and chopped
- 1 tablespoon soft brown sugar
- 30 g (1 oz/$\frac{1}{4}$ cup) sultanas (golden raisins)
- 1 tablespoon shelled pistachio nuts, toasted
- 3 sheets of filo pastry, cut in half
- olive oil spray

Preheat the oven to 180°C (350°F/Gas 4). Line a baking tray with baking paper.

Put the apricots in a bowl and cover with boiling water. Leave for 10 minutes, then drain and roughly chop. Place in a small bowl with the apple, sugar, sultanas and pistachios and mix together well.

Place a half-sheet of filo pastry on a work surface. Spray with olive oil spray, then place another layer on top. Repeat until all six half-sheets are used up. Transfer to the prepared baking tray.

Spoon the apricot mixture along one short edge of the pastry and roll the pastry up, tucking in the ends to seal. Spray the strudel with more olive oil and bake for 25 minutes, or until the pastry is golden.

Cut the strudel into four portions. Serve hot or warm.

serving tip Serve with fresh fruit and low-fat fruit yoghurt

mixed-fruit tea loaf

PER SERVE	
KILOJOULES	694 (165 CAL)
PROTEIN	3.8 g
FAT	3.0 g
SATURATED FAT	0.2 g
CARBOHYDRATE	27.6 g
FIBRE	6.2 g

Serves 12 (makes 12 slices)

Preheat the oven to 180°C (350°F/Gas 4). Lightly grease a loaf (bar) tin and line the base with baking paper.

Put all the dried fruit in a large bowl and pour the hot tea over the top. Cover and leave to stand for 10 minutes.

Remove half the softened apricots and purée them in a blender or food processor with 125 ml (4 fl oz/1/2 cup) of the tea liquid.

Tip the purée back into the mixing bowl. Stir in the banana and orange zest. Combine the flour, baking powder, ground almonds and cinnamon and stir into the fruit mixture.

Pour the mixture into the prepared tin and bake for 45 minutes, or until a skewer inserted into the centre of the loaf comes out clean. Remove from the oven and leave in the tin for 15 minutes, before turning out onto a wire rack to cool.

- 20 dried apricot halves
- 10 dried figs
- 10 pitted prunes
- 5 dried pear halves
- 1 tablespoon raisins
- 500 ml (17 fl oz/2 cups) hot black tea
- 1 banana, mashed
- finely grated zest of 1 orange
- 150 g (51/2 oz/1 cup) wholemeal (whole-wheat) plain (all-purpose) flour
- 2 teaspoons baking powder
- 55 g (2 oz/1/2 cup) ground almonds
- 1 teaspoon ground cinnamon

storage tip Keeps well in the refrigerator, or wrap single-serve portions and freeze them

serving tips The loaf can be toasted and topped with fruit spread. Alternatively, serve with a dollop of low-fat vanilla yoghurt and a sprinkle of cinnamon, or spread with low-fat cream cheese and sliced pear or fresh fig

nutrition tip High in fibre

PER SERVE	
KILOJOULES	968 (230 CAL)
PROTEIN	9.1 g
FAT	8.2 g
SATURATED FAT	3 g
CARBOHYDRATE	28.4 g
FIBRE	3.8 g

peaches with ricotta cream

Serves 4

- 4 large peaches, unpeeled
- 500 ml (17 fl oz/2 cups) unsweetened apple juice
- 1 tablespoon caster (superfine) sugar
- 2 teaspoons lemon juice
- 25 g (1 oz/$1/4$ cup) flaked almonds, lightly toasted

RICOTTA CREAM
- 200 g (7 oz/heaped $3/4$ cup) low-fat ricotta cheese
- 1 teaspoon caster (superfine) sugar
- 1 teaspoon natural vanilla extract
- 1 teaspoon grated lemon zest

Slice each peach in half and remove the stone. Heat the apple juice in a saucepan over medium heat, add the sugar and lemon juice and stir until the sugar has dissolved.

Add the peach halves, then cover and poach over low heat for 5–8 minutes, or until just tender when pierced with a knife. Remove with a slotted spoon and peel away the skins. Reserve the poaching juice and allow the peaches to cool.

Put all the ricotta cream ingredients in a bowl and beat using electric beaters until smooth. Cover with plastic wrap, then refrigerate until firm.

To serve, layer the peach halves and ricotta cream among four serving bowls or glasses, drizzle with the poaching juice, then sprinkle with the flaked almonds.

cook's tip Try poaching other stonefruits such as blood plums, apricots or nectarines

nutrition tip Excellent source of vitamin C

passionfruit bavarois

Serves 8

PER SERVE	
KILOJOULES	654 (156 CAL)
PROTEIN	12.3 g
FAT	4.3 g
SATURATED FAT	1.4 g
CARBOHYDRATE	11.8 g
FIBRE	10.5 g

Push the passionfruit in syrup through a sieve into a small bowl. Discard the seeds, then pour the syrup into a blender. Add the tofu, buttermilk, sugar and vanilla and blend for 90 seconds on high to thoroughly mix. Leave in the blender.

Pour 80 ml (2^1/$_2$ fl oz/^{1}/$_3$ cup) water into a heatproof bowl and sprinkle evenly with the powdered gelatine. Stand the bowl in a saucepan of very hot water and stir until the gelatine has dissolved and the mixture is smooth. Allow to cool slightly.

Place eight 200 ml (7 fl oz) dariole moulds or ramekins in a baking dish. Add the gelatine mixture to the blender and mix on high for 1 minute. Pour into the moulds, cover with plastic wrap and chill overnight.

When ready to serve, carefully run a hot knife around the edge of each mould and dip the bases in very hot water for 2 seconds. Turn each out onto a plate and spoon the passionfruit pulp and strawberry halves around them.

- 2 x 170 g (6 oz) tins passionfruit in syrup
- 300 g (10^1/$_2$ fl oz) silken tofu, chopped
- 600 ml (21 fl oz) buttermilk
- 1 tablespoon caster (superfine) sugar
- 1 teaspoon natural vanilla extract
- 6 teaspoons powdered gelatine
- 185 ml (6 fl oz/^{3}/$_4$ cup) passionfruit pulp
- 250 g (9 oz/1^2/$_3$ cups) strawberries, hulled and cut in half

nutrition tip Excellent source of vitamin C, a good source of calcium and high in fibre

PER SERVE

KILOJOULES	925 (220 CAL)
PROTEIN	7.2 g
FAT	11.2 g
SATURATED FAT	2.3 g
CARBOHYDRATE	21.5 g
FIBRE	2.9 g

grilled figs with sweet ricotta

Serves 4

- 2 tablespoons honey
- 1 cinnamon stick
- 25 g (1 oz/$1/4$ cup) flaked almonds
- 4 large or 8 small fresh figs
- 125 g ($4^1/2$ oz/$1/2$ cup) low-fat ricotta cheese
- $1/2$ teaspoon natural vanilla extract
- 1 tablespoon icing (confectioners') sugar, sifted
- a pinch of ground cinnamon
- $1/2$ teaspoon finely grated orange zest

Put the honey and cinnamon stick in a small saucepan with 80 ml ($2^1/2$ fl oz/$1/3$ cup) water. Bring to the boil, then reduce the heat and simmer gently for 6 minutes, or until the liquid has thickened and reduced by half. Lift out the cinnamon stick with a pair of tongs, then stir in the flaked almonds.

Preheat the grill (broiler) to medium–high. Grease a shallow ovenproof dish that is large enough to fit all the figs side by side. Slice the figs into quarters from the top to within 1 cm ($1/2$ inch) of the bottom, keeping them attached at the base. Arrange in the dish.

In a small bowl, mix together the remaining ingredients. Spoon the mixture into the fig cavities, then spoon the honey syrup over the top. Grill until the juices start to come out from the figs and the almonds are lightly toasted.

Remove from the heat and leave to cool for 2–3 minutes. Spoon the juices and any fallen flaked almonds from the bottom of the dish over the figs and serve.

panna cotta with blueberry compote

Serves 4

PER SERVE	
KILOJOULES	464 (110 CAL)
PROTEIN	7.3 g
FAT	0.2 g
SATURATED FAT	0.1 g
CARBOHYDRATE	14.9 g
FIBRE	1 g

Pour the milk into a heavy-based saucepan. Add the cinnamon stick, vanilla and sugar. Bring to the boil, stirring to dissolve the sugar, then remove from the heat and leave to infuse for 10 minutes.

Soak the gelatine sheets in a bowl of cold water for 5 minutes, or until soft. Squeeze out any excess water and add them to the warm milk mixture. Stir over low heat until the gelatine leaves dissolve — do not allow to boil.

Remove the cinnamon stick from the milk mixture and allow to cool to room temperature. Whisk in the yoghurt. Pour into four 125 ml (4 fl oz/$1/2$ cup) glasses or ramekins and refrigerate for 6 hours, or until set.

Meanwhile, make the blueberry compote. Put the blueberries in a heavy-based saucepan with the sugar, Marsala, lemon peel and cinnamon stick. Cook over low heat for 15 minutes, stirring occasionally and ensuring the fruit does not break up.

Mix the arrowroot with 2 teaspoons water and add to the fruit. Cook, stirring gently, until the mixture has thickened slightly. Pour into a bowl and leave to cool for at least 2 hours.

To serve, remove the cinnamon stick and lemon peel from the blueberry compote and spoon the compote over the panna cotta. If you used ramekins for the panna cotta, run a knife around the edge of each ramekin, invert the panna cotta onto four serving plates and spoon the compote over the top.

- 300 ml (10$1/2$ fl oz) skim milk
- 1 cinnamon stick
- $1/2$ teaspoon natural vanilla extract
- 1 tablespoon caster (superfine) sugar
- 2 sheets of leaf gelatine
- 200 g (7 oz) low-fat vanilla yoghurt

BLUEBERRY COMPOTE
- 150 g (5$1/2$ oz/1 cup) fresh blueberries
- 2 teaspoons caster (superfine) sugar
- 100 ml (3$1/2$ fl oz) Marsala or sherry
- 2 cm ($3/4$ inch) strip of lemon peel, white pith removed
- 1 cinnamon stick
- $1/2$ teaspoon arrowroot

nutrition tip An excellent source of vitamin C, and a good source of calcium

summer pudding

Serves 6

PER SERVE	
KILOJOULES	692 (165 CAL)
PROTEIN	5.6 g
FAT	1.2 g
SATURATED FAT	0.2 g
CARBOHYDRATE	30.5 g
FIBRE	4.1 g

- 600 g (1 lb 5 oz) fresh or frozen mixed berries, such as raspberries, blackberries, redcurrants and blackcurrants
- 200 g (7 oz/1$^1/_3$ cups) strawberries, hulled, then cut into halves or quarters
- 3 tablespoons caster (superfine) sugar
- 6–8 slices of white bread, crusts removed

Put all the fresh or frozen berries except the strawberries in a large saucepan with 125 ml (4 fl oz/$^1/_2$ cup) water. Heat gently for 5 minutes, or until the berries begin to soften. Add the strawberries and remove from the heat. Stir in the sugar and allow to cool.

Use the bread to line six 170 ml (5$^1/_2$ fl oz/$^2/_3$ cup) moulds or a 1 litre (35 fl oz/4 cup) pudding basin (mould). For the small moulds, use one slice of bread for each, cutting a circle to fit the bottoms, and strips to fit snugly around the sides. For the large mould, cut a large circle out of one slice to line the bottom, and cut the rest of the bread into wide fingers to fit around the side.

Drain a little juice from the berries. Dip one side of each piece of bread in the juice before fitting it, juice side down, into the mould or moulds, leaving no gaps. (Do not squeeze or flatten the bread or it will not absorb the juice.) Fill with the berries and add a little juice. Cover with the remaining dipped bread, juice side up (trim the bread to fit if necessary). Cover with plastic wrap.

For the small moulds, sit a tin, or similar weight, on top of each. For the large mould, place a small plate that fits inside the dish onto the plastic wrap, then weigh it down with a large tin. Place on a baking tray and refrigerate overnight. Carefully turn out and serve with any leftover berry mixture.

serving tip Serve with low-fat vanilla yoghurt

nutrition tip Excellent source of vitamin C

spiced poached pears

Serves 6

PER SERVE	
KILOJOULES	637 (152 CAL)
PROTEIN	2.5 g
FAT	0.2 g
SATURATED FAT	0 g
CARBOHYDRATE	24.3 g
FIBRE	4.2 g

Peel, halve and core the pears, then place in a saucepan with the wine, fruit juice and cloves. Using the tip of a sharp knife, slice the vanilla bean in half along its length, then scrape the seeds into the pan. Add the vanilla bean, cinnamon stick and maple syrup. Bring to the boil, then reduce the heat and simmer for 5–7 minutes, or until the pears are tender.

Remove the pan from the heat and cover. Leave the pears to infuse for 30 minutes, then remove with a slotted spoon and place in a serving dish.

Return the syrup to the heat and boil for 6–8 minutes, or until reduced by half. Strain the syrup over the pears. Serve warm or chilled, dolloped with the yoghurt.

- 6 brown pears
- 300 ml (10$\frac{1}{2}$ fl oz) rosé wine
- 150 ml (5 fl oz) apple or pear juice
- 4 cloves
- 1 vanilla bean
- 1 cinnamon stick
- 1 tablespoon maple syrup
- 200 g (7 oz) low-fat vanilla yoghurt

cook's tip Use ricotta cream (see page 154) instead of the yoghurt

white chocolate mousse

Serves 8

PER SERVE	
KILOJOULES	480 (114 CAL)
PROTEIN	7 g
FAT	4.3 g
SATURATED FAT	2.7 g
CARBOHYDRATE	11.3 g
FIBRE	1.7 g

- 100 g (3^1/$_2$ oz/^{2}/$_3$ cup) white chocolate melts (buttons)
- 125 ml (4 fl oz/^{1}/$_2$ cup) skim milk
- 2 teaspoons powdered gelatine
- 400 g (14 oz) low-fat vanilla fromage frais or whipped yoghurt
- 3 egg whites
- 3 tablespoons passionfruit pulp, plus extra, to serve

Bring all the ingredients to room temperature to help ensure the mousse has a smooth texture.

Put the chocolate melts and milk in a small saucepan and stir over low heat until the chocolate has melted. Allow to cool. Pour 60 ml (2 fl oz/^{1}/$_4$ cup) boiling water into a heatproof bowl, sprinkle evenly with the powdered gelatine, then stir until dissolved. Using a wooden spoon, stir the gelatine into the chocolate mixture.

Put the fromage frais in a large bowl and gradually stir in the chocolate mixture, a little at a time, stirring until smooth after each addition.

Beat the egg whites in a clean, dry bowl using electric beaters until soft peaks form. Gently fold into the chocolate mixture with the passionfruit pulp. Divide among eight 125 ml (4 fl oz/ ^{1}/$_2$ cup) serving dishes or a 1 litre (35 fl oz/4 cup) glass bowl. Refrigerate for 3 hours, or until set. Serve garnished with a small dollop of passionfruit pulp.

cook's tip Use fresh raspberries instead of the passionfruit pulp

tiramisu

PER SERVE	
KILOJOULES	650 (155 CAL)
PROTEIN	7.5 g
FAT	3 g
SATURATED FAT	1.5 g
CARBOHYDRATE	23.2 g
FIBRE	0.4 g

Serves 8

Put 2 tablespoons of the milk in a bowl. Stir in the custard powder and sugar, mixing until smooth. Add a little more milk if needed to achieve a smooth consistency.

Pour the remaining milk into a saucepan and add the custard mixture and vanilla. Stir over low heat for 5–6 minutes, or until the custard begins to thicken. Pour into a bowl, cover the surface of the custard with plastic wrap to prevent a skin forming, and leave to cool.

Beat the ricotta and yoghurt together using electric beaters until smooth, then fold into the custard. Beat the egg whites in a clean, dry bowl until soft peaks form, then gently fold into the custard mixture using a metal spoon.

Pour the coffee and Marsala into a bowl and stir. Dip enough of the savoiardi into the coffee to cover the base of a 1.5 litre (52 fl oz/6 cup) rectangular dish. Top with half the custard mixture, then dust with half the cocoa powder. Repeat with the remaining ingredients to form a second layer. Cover and chill for at least 3 hours before serving.

- 250 ml (9 fl oz/1 cup) skim milk
- 2 tablespoons vanilla-flavoured custard powder (instant vanilla pudding mix)
- 1 tablespoon sugar
- 2 teaspoons natural vanilla extract
- 150 g (5$\frac{1}{2}$ oz/scant $\frac{2}{3}$ cup) low-fat ricotta cheese
- 150 g (5$\frac{1}{2}$ oz) low-fat vanilla yoghurt
- 2 egg whites
- 250 ml (9 fl oz/1 cup) black coffee
- 2 tablespoons Marsala or sherry
- 200 g (7 oz) savoiardi (lady fingers/sponge finger biscuits)
- 1$\frac{1}{2}$ tablespoons cocoa powder, sifted

storage tip The tiramisu can be refrigerated for several days

spice it up

Healthy doesn't have to be bland.
Why not marinate, drizzle or dress up
your favourite dish with one of our
fabulous guilt-free flavour boosters?
Feel free to experiment by introducing
different herbs and spices to
keep things 'fresh'.

lemon mint dressing

PER TABLESPOON	
KILOJOULES	41 (10 CAL)
PROTEIN	1.1 g
FAT	0.1 g
SATURATED FAT	0 g
CARBOHYDRATE	1.2 g
FIBRE	0.1 g

Adds a fresh, creamy tang to spicy rice or lentil dishes, or mix through roasted vegetables. Also delicious over sliced lean roast lamb for a modern spin on a traditional dish.

- 250 g (9 oz) plain low-fat yoghurt
- 1 tablespoon lemon juice
- 1 tablespoon chopped mint
- 1/2 teaspoon ground cumin

In a small bowl, mix together all the ingredients and season with freshly ground black pepper.

Makes about 280 ml (9 1/2 fl oz)

basil and garlic dressing

PICTURED PAGE 170 bottom right

A simple dressing to brighten a tossed green salad.

PER TABLESPOON	
KILOJOULES	505 (120 CAL)
PROTEIN	0.1 g
FAT	13.4 g
SATURATED FAT	1.9 g
CARBOHYDRATE	0.4 g
FIBRE	0.1 g

Finely chop the garlic and basil in a food processor or blender. Add the lemon juice and process in short bursts until the mixture has blended. Gradually add the extra virgin olive oil and blend until combined. Season to taste with a little freshly ground black pepper.

Makes about 170 ml (5^1/$_2$ fl oz/^{2}/$_3$ cup)

- 1 garlic clove, peeled
- 2 tablespoons chopped basil
- 3 tablespoons lemon juice
- 125 ml (4 fl oz/^{1}/$_2$ cup) extra virgin olive oil

balsamic syrup

PER TABLESPOON	
KILOJOULES	108 (26 CAL)
PROTEIN	0 g
FAT	0 g
SATURATED FAT	0 g
CARBOHYDRATE	6.3 g
FIBRE	0 g

This simple balsamic reduction is great with grilled chicken or steamed asparagus — and even drizzled over sliced fresh strawberries.

Put the vinegar and sugar in a small saucepan and stir over medium heat until the sugar has dissolved. Reduce the heat and simmer for 3–4 minutes, or until the sauce becomes syrupy. Take off the heat. Serve hot or cold, or cover and refrigerate until required.

Makes about 3 tablespoons

- 4 tablespoons balsamic vinegar
- 1^1/$_2$ tablespoons soft brown sugar

time saver The balsamic syrup can be made a day ahead

tartare sauce

A classic accompaniment for any white-fleshed fish or prawns (shrimp).

- 160 g (5³/₄ oz/²/₃ cup) low-fat mayonnaise
- 1 spring onion (scallion), finely chopped
- 1 tablespoon finely chopped gherkin (pickle)
- 1 tablespoon capers, drained, rinsed and finely chopped
- 1 tablespoon finely chopped parsley
- 2 teaspoons lemon juice

Put all the ingredients in a small, non-metallic serving bowl and mix together well. Cover and refrigerate until required.

Makes about 215 ml (7¹/₂ fl oz)

chinese marinade

PER TABLESPOON	
KILOJOULES	136 (32 CAL)
PROTEIN	0.7 g
FAT	0.5 g
SATURATED FAT	0.1 g
CARBOHYDRATE	5.6 g
FIBRE	0.9 g

Use to marinate cubed firm tofu, chicken, pork or beef strips, or use as a base for a quick stir-fry.

Put all the ingredients in a non-metallic bowl and stir until the sugar has dissolved.

Makes about 185 ml (6 fl oz/³/4 cup)

cook's tip Make it spicy by adding some finely chopped chilli

- 3 tablespoons oyster sauce
- 3 tablespoons hoisin sauce
- 2 tablespoons salt-reduced soy sauce
- 1 tablespoon soft brown sugar
- 3 teaspoons grated fresh ginger
- 3 garlic cloves, crushed

thai chilli marinade

PER TABLESPOON	
KILOJOULES	58 (14 CAL)
PROTEIN	1.1 g
FAT	0.1 g
SATURATED FAT	0 g
CARBOHYDRATE	2.1 g
FIBRE	0.2 g

A tasty marinade for barbecued meats and prawns (shrimp).

Put all the ingredients in a small bowl and stir until the sugar has dissolved.

Makes about 90 ml (3 fl oz)

- 2 tablespoons salt-reduced fish sauce
- 2 tablespoons lime juice
- 1 tablespoon salt-reduced soy sauce
- 2 teaspoons chopped red chilli
- 2 teaspoons soft brown sugar
- 2 tablespoons chopped coriander (cilantro)

almond and red capsicum sauce

PER TABLESPOON	
KILOJOULES	310 (74 CAL)
PROTEIN	1 g
FAT	7.6 g
SATURATED FAT	0.9 g
CARBOHYDRATE	0.5 g
FIBRE	0.5 g

A tasty sauce for beef, chicken and veal dishes, or green vegetables such as asparagus and green beans.

- 1 small red capsicum (pepper), cut into quarters
- 1 garlic clove, unpeeled
- 60 g (2¼ oz/⅔ cup) flaked almonds
- 2 tablespoons red wine vinegar
- 4 tablespoons olive oil
- 1 tablespoon finely chopped parsley

Spread the capsicum on a baking tray, skin side up, and cook under a hot grill (broiler) for 10 minutes. Add the garlic and continue to cook until the capsicum skin blackens and blisters. Place the garlic and capsicum in a plastic bag, allow to cool, then peel away the skins.

Meanwhile, turn the grill down to medium. Spread the almonds on a baking tray and toast under the grill, stirring once or twice, until lightly golden. Set aside to cool for 5 minutes.

Blend the capsicum, garlic and almonds in a food processor until smooth. With the motor running, slowly add the vinegar. Season with freshly ground black pepper. Gradually add the olive oil, then 2 tablespoons boiling water — the sauce should have the consistency of mayonnaise. Add the parsley and process briefly.

Refrigerate for at least 1 hour or preferably overnight to allow the flavours to develop.

Makes about 280 ml (9½ fl oz)

puttanesca sauce

PER 125 g (4½ OZ/½ CUP)	
KILOJOULES	227 (54 CAL)
PROTEIN	1.8 g
FAT	2.1 g
SATURATED FAT	0.3 g
CARBOHYDRATE	6 g
FIBRE	2.1 g

A classic spicy Italian sauce that's perfect for tossing though a pot of steaming hot spaghetti.

- 2 teaspoons olive oil
- 3 garlic cloves, crushed
- 2 tablespoons chopped parsley
- ¼–½ teaspoon chilli flakes or powder
- 2 x 400 g (14 oz) tins no-added-salt chopped tomatoes
- 1 tablespoon capers, drained
- 3 anchovy fillets in oil, drained, thinly sliced, and soaked in a little milk to remove any excess salt
- 40 g (1½ oz/¼ cup) black olives in brine, rinsed, drained, pitted and chopped

Heat the olive oil in a large heavy-based frying pan. Add the garlic, parsley and chilli flakes and stir constantly for 1 minute over medium heat. Stir in the tomato and bring to the boil, then reduce the heat, cover and simmer for 10 minutes.

Add the capers, anchovies and olives. Leave the lid off and simmer, stirring, for another 5 minutes. Season with freshly ground black pepper and serve.

Makes about 750 ml (26 fl oz/3 cups)

cook's tip Spread over a grilled chicken breast fillet and top with grated low-fat mozzarella cheese for a new-style chicken parmigiana

cheese sauce

PER TABLESPOON	
KILOJOULES	78 (19 CAL)
PROTEIN	1.4 g
FAT	0.6 g
SATURATED FAT	0.4 g
CARBOHYDRATE	1.8 g
FIBRE	0 g

Drizzle over steamed or baked vegetables such as broccoli or cauliflower, or use in baked pasta dishes.

In a small saucepan, blend a little of the milk with the cornflour to form a smooth paste. Gradually blend in the remaining milk, add the nutmeg and stir constantly over low heat until the mixture boils and thickens.

Remove from the heat and stir in the cheese until melted. Season to taste with ground white pepper.

Makes about 810 ml (28 fl oz)

- 375 ml (13 fl oz/1^1/$_2$ cups) skim milk
- 2 tablespoons cornflour (cornstarch)
- ^{1}/$_4$ teaspoon ground nutmeg
- 50 g (1^3/$_4$ oz/^{1}/$_3$ cup) grated reduced-fat cheddar cheese

storage tip If you're not using the sauce right away, allow to cool slightly and cover the surface of the sauce with plastic wrap to prevent a 'skin' forming

chilli relish

PER TABLESPOON	
KILOJOULES	89 (21 CAL)
PROTEIN	0.3 g
FAT	0.9 g
SATURATED FAT	0.1 g
CARBOHYDRATE	2.7 g
FIBRE	0.4 g

Delicious as a sandwich relish, or as an accompaniment to steak.

Heat the olive oil in a saucepan. Add the onion, capsicum and garlic and sauté over medium heat for 10 minutes. Stir in the tomato and cook for 5 minutes, then add the chilli, ginger, sugar, balsamic vinegar, salt and some freshly cracked black pepper. Stir until the sugar has dissolved.

Reduce the heat and simmer, uncovered, for 30 minutes, or until the sauce has thickened and bubbles appear on the surface. Remove from the heat, stir in the basil and allow to cool. Transfer to a large sterilized jar and refrigerate.

Makes about 875 ml (30 fl oz/3$^{1}/_{2}$ cups)

- 2 tablespoons olive oil
- 1 red onion, chopped
- 1 red capsicum (pepper), chopped
- 3 garlic cloves, crushed
- 1 x 800 g (1 lb 12 oz) tin crushed no-added-salt roma (plum) tomatoes
- 1 large red chilli, seeded and chopped
- 3 teaspoons grated fresh ginger
- 75 g (2$^{1}/_{2}$ oz/$^{1}/_{3}$ cup) raw (demerara) sugar
- 100 ml (3$^{1}/_{2}$ fl oz) balsamic vinegar
- 1 teaspoon salt
- a handful of basil

storage tip Keeps for up to 1 month in a sterilized jar in the refrigerator

Jenny Craig food groups

All food group calculations are based on the serve size indicated for each recipe. Calculations exclude serving tips.

Start your day

RECIPE	FRUIT	VEGETABLE	GRAIN	MEAT	MILK	FAT	LIMITED FREE
BANANA & OAT PIKELETS	1	0	$3^1/_2$	$^1/_2$	0	$^1/_2$	0
BERRY YOGHURT SMOOTHIE	$^1/_2$	0	0	0	$^1/_2$	0	0
BIRCHER MUESLI	$^1/_2$	0	2	0	1	1	0
CRUNCHY OATS 'N' ALL	1	0	$1^1/_2$	0	$^1/_2$	2	0
ITALIAN-STYLE MINI-OMELETTES	0	0	0	2	0	1	0
MANGO MAPLE SMOOTHIE	1	0	$^1/_2$	0	1	0	0
MIXED-GRAIN PORRIDGE WITH RHUBARB	0	1	3	0	0	0	0
SOURDOUGH TOASTS WITH CRISPY HAM	0	1	2	2	0	0	0
SPINACH & FETA FRITTATAS	0	0	0	1	0	$^1/_2$	0
SWEETCORN & RICOTTA FRITTERS	0	0	$2^1/_2$	2	0	$^1/_2$	0
TROPICAL FRUIT CRUSH	$1^1/_2$	0	0	0	0	0	0

Something light

RECIPE	FRUIT	VEGETABLE	GRAIN	MEAT	MILK	FAT	LIMITED FREE
BEETROOT DIP	0	0	0	0	0	0	1
CLUB SANDWICH 1	0	$^1/_2$	$2^1/_2$	2	0	2	0
CLUB SANDWICH 2	0	$^1/_2$	$2^1/_2$	0	0	$2^1/_2$	0
CREAMY POTATO SOUP	0	0	$2^1/_2$	0	$^1/_2$	$^1/_2$	0
CRUNCHY NOODLE SALAD	0	1	$3^1/_2$	0	0	$2^1/_2$	0
CURRIED VEGETABLE SOUP	0	$1^1/_2$	1	$^1/_2$	0	1	0
EGGPLANT DIP	0	$^1/_2$	0	0	0	$^1/_2$	0
HEARTY CORN SOUP	0	0	2	$^1/_2$	0	$^1/_2$	0
HOMMUS	0	0	$^1/_2$	$^1/_2$	0	1	0
MEDITERRANEAN FISH SOUP	0	2	1	3	0	$^1/_2$	0
MUSHROOM, HAM & OLIVE PIZZA	0	1	2	$1^1/_2$	0	1	0
MUSTARD PRAWNS WITH GARLIC	0	0	0	$2^1/_2$	0	$^1/_2$	0
PROTEIN POWER SALAD	0	$^1/_2$	2	2	0	1	0
RIBOLLITA (TUSCAN BREAD SOUP)	0	$1^1/_2$	$^1/_2$	1	0	$^1/_2$	0
TANDOORI LAMB SALAD	$^1/_2$	1	0	$3^1/_2$	0	0	0
THAI BEEF SALAD	0	$1^1/_2$	$^1/_2$	4	0	1	0
TZATZIKI	0	0	0	0	0	0	1
VIETNAMESE RICE PAPER ROLLS	0	1	2	2 1/2	0	0	0
WARM CHICKEN SALAD	0	1	0	3	0	2	0
WON TONS	0	0	1	2	0	0	0

The main event

RECIPE	FRUIT	VEGETABLE	GRAIN	MEAT	MILK	FAT	LIMITED FREE
ASIAN-STYLE STEAMED FISH	0	0	0	$3^1/_2$	0	1	0
BEEF INVOLTINI	0	2	$1^1/_2$	5	0	0	0
CHARGRILLED TUNA WITH RUBY GRAPEFRUIT SALAD	$1^1/_2$	1	0	$3^1/_2$	0	1	0
CHARGRILLED VEGETABLE PASTA SALAD	0	3	$5^1/_2$	$^1/_2$	0	0	0
CHICKEN A L'ORANGE	0	0	$^1/_2$	4	0	$1^1/_2$	0
CHICKEN & NOODLES WITH HONEY LIME DRESSING	0	1	$2^1/_2$	4	0	0	0
CHICKEN STIR-FRY	0	1	0	4	0	1	0
CHILLI CALAMARI WITH ASIAN SALAD	0	1	$3^1/_2$	3	0	0	0
FRESH VEGETABLE LASAGNE WITH ROCKET	0	2	$3^1/_2$	1	0	1	0
HERB-CRUSTED LAMB ROAST WITH VEGETABLES	0	2	$1^1/_2$	4	0	0	0
HOME-STYLE LENTIL SOUP	0	2	2	3	0	0	0
MADRAS BEEF CURRY	0	0	1	4	0	2	0
MOROCCAN LAMB	0	1	2	5	0	0	0
PEPPERED BEEF ON POTATO MASH	0	2	1	5	0	0	0
POACHED SALMON WITH MANGO SALSA	$^1/_2$	0	0	5	0	2	0
SEAFOOD RISOTTO	0	1/2	$3^1/_2$	3	0	0	0
SIMPLE CHICKEN CASSEROLE	0	$1^1/_2$	1/2	5	0	$1^1/_2$	0
SPRING VEGETABLE RISOTTO	0	1	4	0	0	1	0
STIR-FRIED BEEF & NOODLES	0	$^1/_2$	$4^1/_2$	4	0	1	0
SWEET POTATO & FETA FRITTATA	0	$1^1/_2$	$1^1/_2$	2	$^1/_2$	3	0
TAGLIATELLE WITH SMOKED SALMON & ASPARAGUS	0	1	4	$1^1/_2$	0	1	0
TERIYAKI BEEF WITH CUCUMBER SALAD	0	$^1/_2$	0	4	0	0	0
VEGETARIAN PAELLA	0	$1^1/_2$	3	$1^1/_2$	0	0	0

On the side

RECIPE	FRUIT	VEGETABLE	GRAIN	MEAT	MILK	FAT	LIMITED FREE
ASPARAGUS & GREEN BEANS WITH TOASTED ALMONDS	0	1	0	0	0	1	0
BALSAMIC MUSHROOMS	0	1	0	0	0	$1/2$	0
CARAMELIZED ONIONS ·	0	1	$1/2$	0	0	1	0
GARLIC VEGETABLES	0	1	0	0	0	$1/2$	0
GREEK SALAD	0	2	0	$1/2$	0	$1/2$	0
HASSELBACK POTATOES	0	0	1	0	0	$1/2$	0
HONEYED CARROTS	0	1	$1/2$	0	0	$1/2$	0
ROCKET SALAD	0	2	0	0	0	$1/2$	0
SNOW PEAS & POPPY SEEDS	0	1	0	0	0	$1/2$	0
TOMATO BASIL SALAD	0	2	0	0	0	0	0
ZESTY GREENS	0	1	0	0	0	$1/2$	0

Sweet things

RECIPE	FRUIT	VEGETABLE	GRAIN	MEAT	MILK	FAT	LIMITED FREE
APRICOT & APPLE STRUDEL	1	0	1	0	0	$1/2$	0
FRUIT SALAD WITH GINGER LIME SYRUP	$1 1/2$	0	$1/2$	0	0	0	0
GRILLED FIGS WITH SWEET RICOTTA	1	0	1	$1/2$	0	1	0
MIXED-FRUIT TEA LOAF	$1 1/2$	0	$1/2$	0	0	$1/2$	0
PANNA COTTA WITH BLUEBERRY COMPOTE	$1/2$	0	$1/2$	0	$1/2$	0	0
PASSIONFRUIT BAVAROIS	1	0	$1/2$	$1/2$	0	0	0
PEACHES WITH RICOTTA CREAM	$2 1/2$	0	0	1	0	1	0
SPICED POACHED PEARS	1	0	1	0	0	0	0
SUMMER PUDDING	$1/2$	0	$1 1/2$	0	0	0	0
TIRAMISU	0	0	$1 1/2$	$1/2$	0	0	0
WHITE CHOCOLATE MOUSSE	0	0	1	0	0	1	0

Spice it up

RECIPE	FRUIT	VEGETABLE	GRAIN	MEAT	MILK	FAT	LIMITED FREE	FREE
ALMOND & RED CAPSICUM SAUCE	0	0	0	0	0	1 1/2	0	0
BALSAMIC SYRUP	0	0	0	0	0	0	1	0
BASIL & GARLIC DRESSING	0	0	0	0	0	2 1/2	0	0
CHEESE SAUCE	0	0	0	0	0	0	1	0
CHILLI RELISH	0	0	0	0	0	0	0	1
CHINESE MARINADE	0	0	0	0	0	0	1	0
LEMON MINT DRESSING	0	0	0	0	0	0	1	0
PUTTANESCA SAUCE	0	1	0	0	0	1/2	0	0
TARTARE SAUCE	0	0	0	0	0	0	1	0
THAI CHILLI MARINADE	0	0	0	0	0	0	1	0

Jenny Craig food groups for serving suggestions commonly used throughout this book

1 DINNER ROLL	=	1 GRAIN
1/2 CUP COOKED RICE	=	1 GRAIN
LARGE LEAFY GREEN SALAD	=	1 NON-STARCHY VEGETABLE OR FREE FOOD
1/2 CUP COOKED POTATOES	=	1 GRAIN
1/2 CUP COOKED NOODLES	=	1 GRAIN

index

Recipes and other text contributed by Danielle Bowman, Honi Cervi, Karen Inge,
Karen Kong and Lara Polidori of Jenny Craig

Published in 2007 by Murdoch Books Pty Limited

Murdoch Books Australia
Pier 8/9, 23 Hickson Road
Millers Point NSW 2000
Phone: +61 (0) 2 8220 2000
Fax: +61 (0) 2 8220 2558
www.murdochbooks.com.au

Murdoch Books UK Limited
Erico House, 6th Floor
93–99 Upper Richmond Road
Putney, London SW15 2TG
Phone: +44 (0) 20 8785 5995
Fax: +44 (0) 20 8785 5985
www.murdochbooks.co.uk

Chief executive: Juliet Rogers
Publishing director: Kay Scarlett

Project manager: Tricia Dearborn
Editor: Katri Hilden
Design concept and layout: Vivien Valk
Production: Maiya Levitch
Photography: Tanya Zouev
Stylist for recipes: Simon Bajada
Stylist for incidentals: Janet Mitchell

National Library of Australia Cataloguing-in-Publication Data
Craig, Jenny.
   Jenny Craig: healthy living for life
   Includes index.
   ISBN 978 1 92125 977 7 (pbk.).
   1. Low-fat diet – Recipes. I. Title.
641.563

Colour separation by Splitting Image
Printed by 1010 Printing International Ltd in 2007. Printed in China.

IMPORTANT: The nutritional information provided for each recipe does not include garnishes or accompaniments, such as rice, unless they are included in specific quantities in the ingredients. The values are approximations and can be affected by such factors as biological and seasonal variations in food and the unknown composition of some manufactured foods. The information in this book is not intended to replace any advice about diet and exercise that has been given to you by a health professional. If you have a health condition that requires medical treatment, it is important that you consult your doctor before making any changes to your diet or physical activity program. Those who might be at risk from the effects of salmonella poisoning (the elderly, pregnant women, young children and those suffering from immune deficiency diseases) should consult their doctor with any concerns about eating raw eggs.

CONVERSION GUIDE: You may find cooking times vary depending on the oven you are using. For fan-forced ovens, as a general rule, set the oven temperature to 20°C (35°F) lower than indicated in the recipe. We have used 20 ml (4 teaspoon) tablespoon measures.